5/2000

Sylvia –

The best to you as you lead Academic Affairs at Moraine Valley as the new Vice President. A perfect choice!

Lisa Hinkley

Adult Career Pathways: Providing a Second Chance in Public Education

Compiled and Coauthored
by Richard "Dick" Hinckley
and Dan M. Hull

www.cord.org

For additional copies, contact:

CORD Communications
601 Lake Air Dr.
Waco, Texas 76710
254-776-1822
800-231-3015
Fax 254-776-3906
www.cordcommunications.com

For additional information on implementing Career Pathways, contact:

Teemus Warner, Career Pathways Liaison
601 Lake Air Drive
Waco, Texas 76710
254-772-8756 ext 437
Fax 254-772-8972
twarner@cord.org
www.cord.org

Printed March 2007
Printed July 2008

ISBN 1-57837-447-2 (hardcover); 1-57837-446-4 (softcover)

Contents

The Problem

Our Vision and Strategies

Resources

FOREWORD

As the chancellor of a large community college district in southern California, I take pride in the role our nation's community and technical colleges have played in providing career and technical education. For years, our institutions have led the way in helping students acquire the skills necessary to keep American employers strong and globally competitive.

Through much effort and years of experience, we have learned to meet the needs of traditional-age students. But we have yet to come up with a process that enables us to serve the adults in our communities who are capable of earning post-secondary credentials (certainly at the two-year level) but whose circumstances have thus far prevented them from doing so.

Most of these adults are where they are because—for a wide variety of reasons—they have not taken full advantage of the benefits of public education. Now they need a second chance.

That's what this book is about—providing a second chance in public education to the millions of Americans whose career options are severely limited and likely to remain so unless some outside entity intervenes. The needs of these people are many, and the barriers to their success are often complex, but they are not insurmountable. With the right leadership—and a willingness on the part of educators, employers, community leaders, and policymakers to work together—we can turn things around.

Leadership is the key. College presidents and chancellors as well as CEOs and other organizational leaders at the highest levels must lead the way. We alone have the authority, connections, and resources necessary to bring together entire communities for the shared purpose of providing the second chance that our nation's career-limited adults so desperately need. I urge my colleagues to join me in this important effort.

This book shows how it can be done. It widens the dialogue, raises the bar, and calls us to reach farther than we have reached before. It is a blueprint for success that should be read and reread from cover to cover.

—Dr. Jerome Hunter, Chancellor
North Orange County Community College District, California

INTRODUCTION

Unfortunately, too many of the "Neglected Majority" are still neglected.

As the educational requirements of a rewarding career and fulfilled personal life have risen over the last 30–40 years, the achievement gap between the "haves" and "have nots" has widened. Initiatives such as Tech Prep, contextualized teaching and learning, and small communities have improved the earning and learning potential for many young people in the middle 65 percent of the educational spectrum, but huge numbers still enter adulthood without the educational credentials necessary to raise themselves and their families above the poverty level. The fault for the failures of public education lies with dysfunctional families, schools, and communities—and, yes, the individuals themselves. There's plenty of blame to go around. But pointing fingers is futile. We have a problem on our hands, and we must find a way to fix it. With each passing day, more of our young adults become economic liabilities and, in some cases, threats to our society.

The career limitations of our young people are only one side of the coin. The other is that employers throughout our country face a diminishing pool of workers who are qualified for the critical jobs needed to keep America's private sector competitive in today's global economy. Many businesses are being forced to outsource jobs to workers in other countries. If that trend continues unchecked, the future of our nation is in jeopardy.

We believe that the key to providing a better life for millions of Americans, and giving our employers a strong home-grown workforce, is an educational strategy called Career Pathways. In 2005, coauthor Dan Hull and a group of twenty experts from around the country produced a thorough treatment of Career Pathways titled *Career Pathways: Education with a Purpose* (CORD). That book provides the following definition:

> *A Career Pathway is a coherent, articulated sequence of rigorous academic and career/technical courses, commencing in the ninth grade and leading to an associate degree, baccalaureate degree and beyond, an industry-recognized certificate, and/or licensure.*

Whereas the book cited above focuses primarily on high school students on their way up, this book focuses on adults in need of a second chance. We extend the Career Pathways concept by giving it an adult focus. Our working definition is this:

> *An Adult Career Pathway (ACP) consists of the guidance, remediation, curricula, and other support elements required to enable career-limited adults to enter the workforce and progress in rewarding careers.*

This book is a "call to action." It challenges educators, community leaders, and businesspeople to work together in finding a solution to a problem that prevents many U.S. citizens from obtaining the education that today's workplace demands. Current federal, state, and community programs are not solving the problem.

We propose a fresh and challenging plan with practical strategies to tackle this urgent need. Chapter 1 presents the scope and magnitude of the problem. Chapters 2 and 3 set forth a solution. Chapters 4–8 offer strategies, based on experiences and practices of community college leaders who are trying to address the problem. Chapter 9 considers the costs while Chapters 10 and 11 examine existing policies and programs at the federal and state levels.

Public resources alone will not provide enough to support ACP programs, so Chapter 12 explores the resources (both financial and "in-kind") that must to come from the private sector and from the businesses and other organizations that stand to benefit from having adequate supplies of world-class workers in their communities.

We urge community college presidents, community leaders, and CEOs to begin the dialog about Adult Career Pathways as soon as possible.

Dick Hinckley and Dan Hull
April 2007

ACKNOWLEDGMENTS

Adult Career Pathways are very different from the largely secondary-focused Career Pathways (4+2) or Tech Prep that was described in the forerunner to this book—*Career Pathways: Education with a Purpose* (CORD, 2005). Yes, Adult Career Pathways are still about career and technical education, the Neglected Majority, and the need for world-class workers. But many of the adult student's characteristics, personal needs, and motivations are greatly different from those of high school students; the community college curricula are different; and the participation by employers and community leaders has to be at a much higher level.

Fortunately, the backgrounds and experience of the two of us are complementary. Early on in this book's development we realized that we would need to rely much more on other postsecondary practitioners and employers who were experienced in working with these adult groups.

The data from Mark Whitney's research, described in Chapter 1, helped us to understand the scope of the problem—enormous! Growing out of this, we developed a vision of what needs to be done, but found no complete model programs in the field to refer to. So last summer we decided to write up our ideas in a monograph and to seek reactions. In the early fall we distributed the monograph to six employers and six community college presidents and chancellors. They endorsed the concept enthusiastically and offered suggestions for improvement.

We used this input to refine the monograph and then distributed 3000 copies at the November 2006 National Tech Prep Conference in Dallas. We also held three focus groups at the conference, receiving more encouragement and suggestions. As we prepared the manuscript, we drew on the expertise and experience of the generous professionals listed on the back cover of this book. This book embodies excellent contributions and combined wisdom of all the groups named above—and more. To all who have contributed, we express our sincere gratitude.

Dan and Dick
April 2007

CONTRIBUTORS

DAVID BOND, ED.D., is CORD's Senior Vice President for Career Pathways and also Director of the National Tech Prep Network. He has been with CORD since 1993. Prior to that Dr. Bond served as a U.S. Army officer and as an administrator at Missouri Baptist College and at Baylor University. He has directed 14 national conferences, conducted statewide and local evaluations on program effectiveness, made several presentations at education conferences, and written numerous articles for the NTPN *Connections* newsletter, and was a contributing author to *Career Pathways: Education with a Purpose.*

MICHAEL BRUSTEIN is a nationally recognized authority on the federal role in education and has spent the past 32 years concentrating on the federal delivery system for career and technical education. He is a founding partner in the Washington, D.C., law firm Brustein & Manasevit, which maintains a nationwide education practice. He has authored and coauthored several books on career and technical education, Tech Prep, and workforce development.

KATHY D'ANTONI, ED.D., is Vice Chancellor for the West Virginia Community and Technical College System. Her career in education includes teaching positions as well as working with the Tech Prep initiative at Marshall University and serving as West Virginia's State Director for Tech Prep. Dr. D'Antoni has worked extensively with curriculum alignment and development projects and is the past president of the National Association for Tech Prep Leadership. She has authored numerous articles on effective transitions from public schools to higher education.

HOLLY ANN DOUGHTY is a research associate and curriculum developer at CORD, where she has worked on both local and international curriculum projects. Before joining CORD in 2006, she was involved in public education as a classroom teacher and as a curriculum writer for the Instructional Materials Service at Texas A&M University.

PAMELA GIST is the Executive Dean of Liberal Arts at Cedar Valley College in Lancaster, Texas, where she manages a division consisting of 19 academic programs, 26 full-time faculty members, and over 50 adjunct faculty members. In a former position of Dean of Resource Development, she developed successful grants that contributed more than $20 million to campus programs. Other positions have included Director of Special Populations, Director of TRIO, Director of Perkins funding, and Coordinator of Tutoring. Throughout her administrative career, she has continued to teach college-level English courses and to advocate for students in all that she does. She is also a trained Formation Facilitator and works with the National Center for Formation in the Community College in Dallas, Texas.

RICHARD HINCKLEY, PH.D., has served public education as a teacher, principal, superintendent, and college dean. He spent his early career with the Illinois Department of Corrections as a teacher and principal in the juvenile division and as superintendent of schools for both the adult and juvenile divisions. He served Moraine Valley Community College in Palos Hills, Illinois, as dean of workforce development and community services and dean of business and industrial technology. At Moraine Valley, he led the formation of the local Tech Prep consortium and managed related grant programs. Hinckley was instrumental in the creation of one of the earliest advanced technology centers (ATC) and, in 2000, became executive director of the National Coalition of Advanced Technology Centers (NCATC). In July 2006, he became the new president and CEO of CORD.

DANIEL HULL, P.E., has spent over thirty years leading education reform efforts across the United States and internationally. He is one of the founding architects of Tech Prep and is among the nation's foremost experts on technical education and workforce development. For over two decades he served as president and CEO of CORD, a national nonprofit research and development organization, and is currently director of OP-TEC: The National Center for Optics and

Photonics Education, funded through the National Science Foundation's Advanced Technological Education (ATE) program. A registered professional engineer, Hull received the National Association of State Directors of Career Technical Education's Distinguished Service Award. He is the author of four books on Tech Prep and contextual teaching and coauthor of the recent book *Career Pathways: Education with a Purpose* (CORD, 2005).

ANTHONY J. IACONO, PH.D., is the Associate Dean of Developmental Education at Indian River Community College (IRCC), where he has worked since 1999. His administrative responsibilities include operation of IRCC's College Prep program, tutorial centers, and student assessment centers. He also serves on a number of state educational committees that explore new ways to help at-risk students.

FRANK JENNINGS, CPA, has been CORD's chief financial officer since 1994. He has extensive experience in developing and tracking budgets and in auditing secondary and postsecondary educational institutions. In his years at CORD, he has provided financial oversight for many large projects, including projects with international clients.

DEBRA MILLS serves as CORD's Vice President for Partnerships. Her focus areas include secondary-to-postsecondary transitions, curriculum development (4+2), staff development, linkages between secondary and postsecondary institutions, and business-education partnerships. Mills has delivered numerous keynote speeches at state education conferences. She is part of the *College & Career Transition Leadership Team* (OVAE Project) and was a contributing author to *Career Pathways: Education with a Purpose*.

BONNIE RINARD is a research associate at CORD, where she has worked on numerous curriculum development projects over the past 28 years. She was project director for the development of CORD's *Applications in Biology/Chemistry* curriculum and served as an educational specialist in the development of *CORD Biology*. She has worked on curriculum projects in math, physics, fossil fueled power plant technology, construction, engineering, and biotechnology. Related areas of expertise include contextual teaching and learning, standards-based curriculum, authentic assessment strategies, project-based learning, and integrated learning.

JOHN SOUDERS, PH.D., is the Director of Curriculum for OP-TEC: The National Center for Optics and Photonics Education. In this role, he has the responsibility of developing programs and curriculum materials that generate highly qualified workers for supporting the Unites States' photonics industry. Previous to this position, he was the Interim Vice President for Student and Academic Affairs and Executive Dean of Liberal Arts at Cedar Valley College. Dr. Souders served six years at CORD as the Senior Vice President for Curriculum Materials. During his tenure, he led several mathematics and science projects producing such titles as *CORD Algebra, CORD Bridges*, and *CORD Geometry*. Dr. Souders taught physics for 11 years at the United States Air Force Academy where he held the rank of full professor.

MARK WHITNEY, PH.D., is CORD's Manager of Publication Services. In that capacity he has provided editorial control and quality assurance on hundreds of CORD documents, including curriculum materials (both printed and online), reports, surveys, proposals, books, and articles.

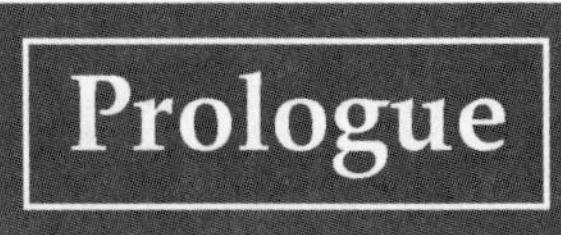

Career-Limited Adults in the Era of High Technology and Globalization

Jesse struggled in school. By the time he was in the fifth grade, it was apparent to him, and everyone else, that he wasn't a "high achiever." When he entered middle school, things got worse. Math didn't make sense, he didn't like his reading assignments, and he had a hard time organizing his writing and "getting started." By the time he entered the eighth grade, Jesse was starting to question why he was still in school, why he needed to learn things that he would probably never use, and whether there wasn't something else he could be doing that he would like better than school.

But then things began to improve for Jesse. During the eighth grade Jesse learned about different jobs, discovered his career interests and abilities, and found out that he could choose school subjects that helped him explore and prepare for a future in an interesting career area. Jesse chose to enroll in an IT academy in high school. In the eleventh grade, he switched to an engineering academy. By the time he graduated from high school, he had already earned 12 hours of dual credit through a nearby college, had earned a scholarship, and was well on his way to becoming a photonics engineering technician. Jesse enjoyed the benefits of Career Pathways!

Karla's experience in school didn't turn out as well. As with Jesse, her low performance in academic subjects was matched by her low self-esteem. By the time she reached high school, her mind was somewhere else. Her only goal in school was just to "get out." She took the easiest path, barely graduating. Although she avoided getting into serious trouble, she left school without a plan and without much preparation for a future. She got a job waiting tables, got married within a year, gave birth to a child, and began to "grow up." Within a few years, she became a single mother and had to return home to live with her parents, because she didn't have the resources or support structures to "handle life" on her own.

Karla was 24 years old and without much of a future before her. Yes, she has made some bad choices. But she was also the failure of our public education system. She wants a second chance at education, a career, and a more rewarding life – and we have a responsibility to help her get it! ♦

These two scenarios reflect the experiences of two large groups of students in U.S. public education. Students in the group represented by Jesse have benefited from their educational experience – and so has the economic competitiveness of our nation. They will get and keep good jobs, and they're prepared for career changes and additional education and training. They're the beneficiaries of successful Career Pathways.

Students like Karla just didn't "get it" when they were in school. Whether the fault lies in a mismatch between learning and teaching styles, a lack of career awareness and career foundations, poor self-image, or just plain immaturity, the students in this group represent a failure of public education and community support – and we have a responsibility to give them a "second chance" in education. So far, this responsibility has fallen on our community and technical colleges, and those institutions should and will continue to play a huge role in "second-chance" education. But more is needed. We need a more systematic approach that involves collaboration between business and education and helps adults balance the demands of family commitments and work as they get back on track in education and careers. The approach we envision is an extension of Career Pathways that caters specifically to the needs of adults. We call it Adult Career Pathways (ACP).[1]

Every American who needs and wants a "second chance" in public education should get one. The reasons should be obvious. American businesses cannot succeed without a well-educated workforce, and our communities need responsible, contributing, financially independent citizens. But, most of all, every person in the United States of America should have the right to improve and to realize his or her dreams. And a high-quality, focused public education is still the key to ensuring that every American enjoys that right.

Over the last thirty years, our society has redefined what constitutes a high-quality, focused public education.

1. Public education should still focus on mastery of core academic subjects such as reading, writing, mathematics, science, and social studies. But today, the academics should be *useful*—not just "math for math's sake" or math to learn more math, but math that can be applied to the real problems that confront us in life and work. The ability to use computers and the Internet is also becoming a foundational academic requirement.
2. Public education should teach social and interpersonal skills and should give students the tools and the desire to produce high-quality work. These are not merely "life skills," they're essential to effectiveness in the workplace. Today's employers value "soft skills" as much or more than career-specific technical skills.
3. Public education should provide a *career foundation*—the basic knowledge and skills that are necessary not only to get a job but also to continue to learn and advance in one's career.

---

[1] For a thorough discussion of Career Pathways, see Dan Hull et al., *Career Pathways: Education with a Purpose* (CORD, 2005).

4. Public education at the secondary level should lead naturally and seamlessly to at least two years of postsecondary education. In most career areas, a high school education alone is not sufficient to create opportunities for high-quality life and work. Nearly all rewarding careers require some form of education beyond high school. To be in demand and upwardly mobile in the workplace, most adults will have to engage in a lifelong pursuit of education and training. *Learning to learn* is vital.

Unfortunately, many of today's young people are entering adulthood (or are well into adulthood) without this type of education. Included in this group are:

1. High school dropouts;
2. High school completers who did not pursue further education and training;
3. College noncompleters;
4. Foreign-born U.S. residents (especially recent Mexican immigrants);
5. Veterans who entered military service immediately following high school; and
6. Criminal offenders who have completed their terms of incarceration.[2]

> For the purpose of this book, "Adult Career Pathways" (ACP) is defined as the guidance, remediation, curricula, and other support elements required to enable career-limited adults to enter the workforce and progress in rewarding careers.

---

[2] There is another category of adults who require retraining or continuing education to change careers, reenter the workforce, or advance in their present careers. In a future book we will define an educational plan for this category as "Career Pathways for Retooling Adults."

The Problem

Profiles of Adults in Need of a Second Chance in Public Education

Mark Whitney

The central premise of this book is that many adult Americans are capable of making good lives for themselves and their families but have stopped far short of their potential. Because of financial obligations, a lack of up-to-date technical and employability skills, and/or weak academic foundations, they feel that the door to a better life is closed to them. They need help in overcoming barriers to self-improvement. We believe that Adult Career Pathways (ACP) can play a vital role in helping to remove those barriers. The connection between education and earnings is well established. On average, the more education a person has, the more in-demand he or she is in the workplace. ACP programs have the potential to help those struggling adults make significant strides forward in the workplace, in their communities, and in their personal lives.

This chapter presents profiles of the six groups of career-limited adults cited in the prologue. Obviously, the six groups sometimes overlap. Many ex-offenders, for example, are high school dropouts, and many recently returned veterans have only a high school diploma or GED. But by focusing on these groups, we hope to identify the most urgent needs that affect our nation's struggling adults. It is in these areas especially that the implementation of Career Pathways could provide a vital second chance.

As we develop our profiles of the six targeted groups, we will return often to several basic questions. For example, how large are the groups? Are the numbers growing? Are career limitations worse among particular ethnic groups or in certain places? How are the needs of the different groups already being met?

HIGH SCHOOL DROPOUTS

For several years the federal government reported the national high school graduation rate at just under 90 percent, based on information provided by the Census Bureau. In meeting the reporting requirement for the No Child Left Behind Act (NCLB), the states have painted a similarly optimistic picture. But in the last four years, independent researchers have concluded that far fewer high school students are graduating than had previously been thought. Researchers such as Jay P. Greene of the Manhattan Institute for Policy Research and Christopher Swanson of the Urban Institute have argued that self-reported data provided to the Census Bureau are probably not completely reliable, and that GED recipients should *not* be counted as high school graduates, since the process of obtaining a high school diploma and the process of passing the GED are quite different. By comparing the number of eighth graders for a given year to the number of high school diplomas awarded five years later, or by comparing the 17-year-old population for a given year to the number of high school diplomas awarded the *same* year, these researchers have arrived at national graduation rates variously reported between 66 and 71 percent (Barton, 2005).[1] In other words, the dropout problem may be affecting as much as a third of our student population.

---

[1] For a summary of calculation methods, see Barton, 2004, 44ff.

Bear in mind that those are *national averages*. The graduation rates among some minorities are much lower. According to some estimates, only about half of African American and Hispanic students graduate (Bridgeland, DiIluio, & Morison, 2006; Orfield, 2004), fewer still among males. High dropout rates tend also to be associated with low socioeconomic status and with large urban populations (Balfanz & Letgers, 2004). Among the nation's ten largest school systems, the overall graduation rate is less than 40 percent (Greene and Winters, 2006).

So, if it is true that only about two thirds of American high school students graduate, how many people are directly affected by this problem? According to Martin and Halperin (2006):

> In 2004, there were 27,819,000 18-24-year-olds in the United States. Of these, 21,542,000 (78%) had either graduated from high school, earned a GED, completed some college, or earned an associate or bachelor's degree. The balance, 6,277,000 (22%), had not yet completed high school. Some scholars exclude GED holders, resulting in a much higher noncompletion figure. Similarly, if researchers count the adult population over age 24, the high school noncompletion rate would be higher still.

Snapshot

High School Dropouts

How many? Over 6 million; more if GEDs are excluded and older adults are included

Ethnic makeup: Disproportionately minority (The graduation rate for minorities has been estimated at around 50%.)

Gender: More males than females

Family status: Many from low-income and single-parent homes

Services currently available: Job Corps, YouthBuild, Service Corps, Challenge, AmeriCorps, Workforce Investment Act, Youth Opportunity Grants

Special problems: Lack of family support system; lack of literacy, technical, and employability skills

Special needs: Remediation, employability skills, core academic and technical skills

Despite the magnitude of the dropout problem, opportunities for high school dropouts to resume education and training are diminishing. In the late 1970s, federal spending for second-chance programs was about $15 billion. In 2005 it was closer to $3 billion (Barton, 2005). The ill effects of the dropout problem are compounded by two related facts: (1) Because of the growing complexity of today's high-tech workplace, the earning potential of high school dropouts is steadily declining. (2) Today's recent high school dropouts are younger than in times past. Whereas three decades ago, most dropping out occurred between grades 11 and 12, today students typically drop out between grades 9 and 10, which means that, on average, today's dropouts enter adulthood with even less education and experience than those of the previous generation (Barton, 2005).

High school dropouts who want to go back and obtain credentials are served by several programs such as the Job Corps, Youthbuild USA, the Center for Employment Training, and, of course, the GED. But, as reported by the Campaign for Youth:

> All of the full-time federally funded education, employment, and national service programs combined (Job Corps, YouthBuild, Service Corps, Challenge, AmeriCorps, Workforce Investment Act, Youth Opportunity Grants) are barely scratching the surface of the need and demand. There are less than 300,000 full-time training and educational opportunities for 2.4 million low-income 16 to 24 year-olds who left school without a diploma or got a diploma and can't find work. *(Quoted in Barton, 2005)*

Each year thousands of high school dropouts turn to the GED as a means of getting back on track, but the benefits of the GED are limited. Studies of GED passers have shown that the greatest benefit of the credential is that it enables one to pursue postsecondary education opportunities. With respect to its impact on success in later life, it should not be considered a substitute for a high school diploma. Based on a synthesis of research on the effects of GED completion, Boesel et al. (1998) concluded that

> In some respects, GED recipients resemble high school graduates; in others, they resemble dropouts; in still other ways, they fall between the two. Given these mixed findings,

the common practice of counting GEDs as high school graduates in educational statistics should be reconsidered.

From an economic standpoint, most of today's recent high school dropouts are headed for a life of sporadic employment and relatively low wages. Many will struggle to set up stable households. Among minorities, the outlook is even more grim. For example, among African Americans in the 16-to-24 age group who are not in school and lack high school diplomas, only 35 percent are currently employed (Barton, 2005).

It would be easy to assume that many high school dropouts are destined to second-class status because of a lack of *ability*, but this would be a wrong assumption. The conventional teaching methods that pervade our high schools do not speak to the diversity of student learning styles. Surveys of high school dropouts point to many reasons for dropping out, from lack of parental involvement to a wide variety of personal problems. But fewer than half report dropping out because of significant academic challenges (Bridgeland, DiIluio, & Morison, 2006). Clearly, our nation's population of high school dropouts represents a vast pool of human potential that remains to be tapped.

HIGH SCHOOL COMPLETERS WITH NO COLLEGE

In 1988, Samuel Halperin of the William T. Grant Foundation Commission on Work, Family, and Citizenship produced two landmark reports on the (at that time) twenty million American young people who had chosen *not* to go to college (Halperin, 1988a,b). In both reports, Halperin referred to the target demographic as "the Forgotten Half"—forgotten because, as he put it,

> educators have become so preoccupied with those who go on to college that they have lost sight of those who do not. And more and more of the non-college-bound now fall between the cracks when they are in school, drop out, or graduate inadequately prepared for the requirements of the society and the workplace. (Halperin, 1988a)

Most students who plan to go to college can obtain some form of financial aid, if only in the form of government subsidies on student loans. But students who do *not* plan to attend college usually get no help at all in making the transition from school to the workplace. Federally supported job training programs are woefully inadequate to meet the demand, and many students in the Forgotten Half face personal barriers that more traditional college-bound students do not (Halperin 1988a). As a result, young people in the Forgotten Half of 1988 struggled to find "jobs with a future," were frequently unemployed, and were experiencing steep declines in real income.

A decade after Halperin's first reports came out, he led a team of experts and commentators in the production of a follow-up study titled *The Forgotten Half Revisited: American Youth and Young Families, 1988–2008* (Halperin, 1998). In the follow-up study, Halperin concluded that in key areas the situation had changed very little over the intervening ten years. Whereas in 1988, about 28 percent of Americans age 16 and over had high school diplomas or GEDs but no college, the percentage ten years later was only slightly higher (31.4). Young people in the Forgotten Half were still employed at relatively low rates. Among young people with high school diplomas but no college, the employment rates were 76.5 percent for whites, 70 percent for Hispanics, and a scant 59.5 percent for African Americans. On average, one out of four could not earn enough to rise above the poverty line. Educational attainment continued to be strongly influenced by

Snapshot

High School Completers with No College

How many? 1.5 million per year (derived by subtracting the number of first-time college enrollees from the number of high school graduates [source: NCES])

Ethnic makeup: Disproportionately minority

Family status: Disproportionately from low-income households

Services currently available: Community colleges and technical schools (which offer credential programs that can be completed in as little as one year)

Special problems: Poverty, unemployment or underemployment

Special needs: Advanced (postsecondary-level) skills

family income, and in several measures, minorities continued to lag significantly behind their white counterparts.

Jennings and Rentner, contributors to *The Forgotten Half Revisited,* found reasons for cautious optimism in the general rise in the number of young Americans who attend college (as described in the following section). As a result of that trend, they argued, the Forgotten Half had become a Forgotten *Third,* in the sense that only about a third of high schools graduates decide *not* to pursue college. The bad news, they claimed, was that "the ones left behind—those who do not gain any education or training beyond high school and those who do not even earn a high school degree—face a bleaker economic future than 'The Forgotten Half' of the 1980s" (Jennings & Rentner, 1998).

Without some well-designed intervention, the bleak future faced by the millions of America's young adults who lack *any* postsecondary education is unlikely to change in the foreseeable future. In a ten-year employment projection covering the years 2000 to 2010, the *Monthly Labor Review* stated that "occupations requiring a postsecondary vocational award or an academic degree, which accounted for 29 percent of all jobs in 2000, will account for 42 percent of total job growth from 2000 to 2010" (Hecker, 2001).

COLLEGE NONCOMPLETERS

Over the past several decades, the percentage of America's young people who enter college in the fall immediately following high school graduation has been rising. According to statistics published by the U.S. Census Bureau, almost every demographic has made significant strides in college enrollment. Whereas in 1975 fewer than half of high school graduates enrolled in two- and four-year colleges, by 2001 almost two out of three did so (Table 1-1).

That's good news. But the general upturn in college-going rates has tended to mask a serious problem: Far too few of the students who enroll in America's colleges and universities succeed in earning postsecondary credentials (Table 1-2). Even among students who would seem to have the best chances of success—i.e., those who begin their college careers as full-time freshmen in four-year colleges and universities—only about three out of five obtain bachelor's degrees within six years (Berkner, He, & Cataldi, 2002). In real numbers, that trend represents over half a million students each year (Carey, 2004). This is consistent with the reporting of Schemo (2006), who states that "nearly half the 14.7 million undergraduates at two- and four-year institutions never receive degrees."

Table 1-1. More Students from All Groups Are Going to College

	Immediate College Enrollment Rates (3-year avg)		
	1975	**2001**	**Change in % points**
Total	49%	63%	+14
Low-Income	31%	48%	+17
African Am.	45%	56%	+11
Latino	53%	53%	0
White	49%	66%	+17
Men	53%	62%	+9
Women	49%	68%	+19

(Source: U.S. Census Bureau, CPS, after Carey, 2004)

Table 1-2. College Graduation Rates (within Six Years of Initial Enrollment)

Total	63%
Low-Income	54%
High-Income	77%
African American	46%
Latino	47%
White	67%
Men	59%
Women	66%

(Source: Berkner, He, & Cataldi, 2002, after Carey, 2004)

According to some studies, the noncompletion *percentages* are not rising. The real problem is that the *consequences* of noncompletion have become more severe. In times past, American college noncompleters could be reasonably confident of finding mid-level jobs with opportunities for career advancement. But globalization has made it increasingly difficult for college noncompleters to keep pace with the competition. Moreover, because of advances in telecommunication, it is now possible to "offshore" a wide range of white collar jobs to foreign countries—and that is happening at an alarming rate (Friedman, 2005). As a result, American college noncompleters find themselves at the lower end of a steadily growing gap between their earnings and the earnings of college graduates. As Figure 1-1 shows, holders of bachelor's and advanced degrees have made considerable progress over the past quarter century, while college noncompleters ("some college" in the chart) have made relatively little.

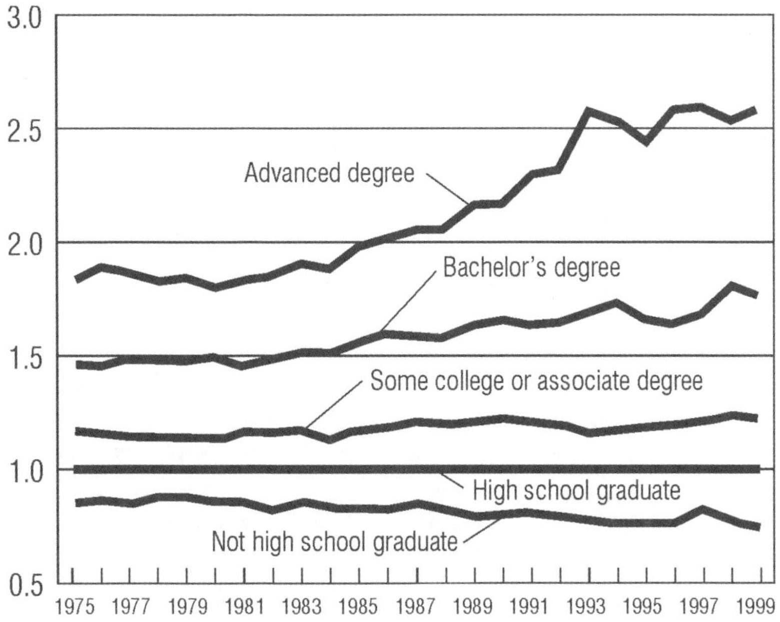

Figure 1-1. Average Earnings of Full-Time, Year-Round Workers as a Proportion of the Average Earnings of High School Graduates by Educational Attainment: 1975 to 1999
(Source: Day & Newburger, 2002)

The extent of the problem can also be seen in the sheer numbers of people involved. According to the latest U. S. Census numbers, within the 25–34 age group, those categorized as "some college, no degree" account for 19 percent (Carey, 2004). In other words, every year hundreds of thousands of America's young people leave college without having completed degree programs. Considering that many have taken on student loans, the sad fact is that some are worse off when they leave school than they were when they started.

The college noncompleter demographic is disproportionately represented by low-income and minority students (National Center for Public Policy and Higher Education, 2004). By age 26, only about 7 percent of all lower-income students have earned bachelor's degrees, compared to 60 percent for upper-income students. The gap between the graduation rates of African American and white students is about 10 percent. Hispanic students also lag behind their white counterparts. Among postsecondary institutions with Hispanic populations of at least 5 percent, one fourth have graduation rates of 30 percent or less. The Hispanic "graduation gap" is typically about 7 percent; about a fourth of schools have gaps of 15 percent or more (Carey, 2004).

Snapshot

College Noncompleters

How many? 0.5 million students per year (Carey, 2004); 19% of total population age 25–34 (= 7,600,000, using Census Bureau figures)

Ethnic makeup: Disproportionately minority

Gender: More men than women; gender gap more pronounced among minorities

Family status: Disproportionately low-income

Services currently available: None specifically for this group

Special problems: Underemployment

Special needs: Means of dealing with personal commitments while going back to school

In general, the picture for students at community colleges is even less optimistic than that for students at four-year colleges and universities. According to the National Center for Education Statistics, "compared with students who started at 4-year institutions, those who started at public 2-year institutions were less well prepared for college and were less likely to be continuously enrolled. Beginners at public 2-year institutions were also more likely to enroll part time, to have delayed enrolling after high school, and to be nontraditional students starting postsecondary education with one or more persistence risk factors" (Berkner, He, & Cataldi, 2002).

College noncompleters leave college for a variety of reasons. Many experience financial difficulties; many struggle academically. Those who study technical fields are sometimes lured away by employers. On the surface this may not seem a serious problem, since one reason for going to college is to become employable. But young people who accept the short-term rewards of employment risk missing out on the long-term benefits of completing their programs of study. When young adults enter the workforce prematurely, their limited skills can quickly be outpaced by the demands of the workplace, leaving them little opportunity for advancement.

FOREIGN-BORN U.S. RESIDENTS (ESPECIALLY RECENT MEXICAN IMMIGRANTS)

According to the U.S. Census Bureau, in 2003, 33.5 million U.S. residents were foreign born (representing 11.7 percent of the total U.S. population). The Census Bureau recognizes four broad geographical regions of foreign nativity: Europe, Asia, Latin America, and "other." Of those four, by far the greatest "sending" region is Latin America (representing 53.3 percent of all foreign-born U.S. residents). The Census Bureau recognizes three subregions within Latin America: the Caribbean, Central America, and South America. Of those three, Central America (which includes Mexico) accounts for over two thirds (69 percent) of all foreign-born U.S. residents of Latin American nativity (U.S. Census Bureau, 2004). Among Central American countries, Mexico sends (by far) the largest number of people. Today approximately 10 million of the United States' foreign-born residents came from Mexico (Greico, 2003).

In developing Adult Career Pathways for foreign-born residents, there are several reasons to narrow our focus to Hispanics, especially those who come from Mexico.

1. Of all foreign-born subgroups, Hispanics are by far the largest group and Mexicans the largest subgroup.
2. The *pace* of Hispanic immigration is rapidly increasing. The number of foreign-born U.S. residents from Mexico doubled from 1990 to 2000 and is now ten times what it was in 1970 (Camarota, 2001; Greico, 2003). Over a third of Mexican immigrants have come since 2000. As a result, the Hispanic population in the United States is the fastest growing segment of the population, soon to outnumber African Americans (U.S. Census Bureau, 2003, 2004).
3. The distribution of Hispanic immigrants is becoming national in scope. Over the past two decades the highest concentrations of Hispanic immigrants have been located in six states: Arizona, California, Florida, Illinois, New Jersey, and Texas. Today several other states (e.g., Tennessee, Alabama, Georgia, and North Carolina) have burgeoning Hispanic populations. No state's Hispanic population has decreased or stagnated.
4. Most Hispanic immigrants have their most potentially productive years still ahead of them. In other words, they

Snapshot

Foreign-Born Residents

How many? 33.5 million (in 2003)

Ethnic makeup: 53.3% Latin American; 25.0% Asian; 13.7% European; 8.0% Other; largest single group is Mexican (approx 10 million)

Family status: Compared to native population, tend to have large families and (among Hispanics) are more likely to be relatively low in education and socioeconomic factors.

Services currently available: Title I and II of WIA, Refugee Resettlement Program, TANF, HEA; many (but not enough) community colleges and nonprofit organizations offer ESL programs.

Special problems: Especially among Hispanics (of which people born in Mexico are the largest subgroup): Many lack high school diplomas; many lack the resources to move beyond low-paying jobs

Special needs: Remediation, language training, information about career options, high-level skills

are a relatively young group (U.S. Census Bureau, 2002) (Figure 1-2).

5. Because of their large numbers, Hispanic immigrants stand to play a huge role in the future growth of the American workforce. According to some estimates, foreign-born workers will account for *all* of the growth in the American workforce in the 25- to 54-year-old range over the next two decades (Aspen Institute, 2002).

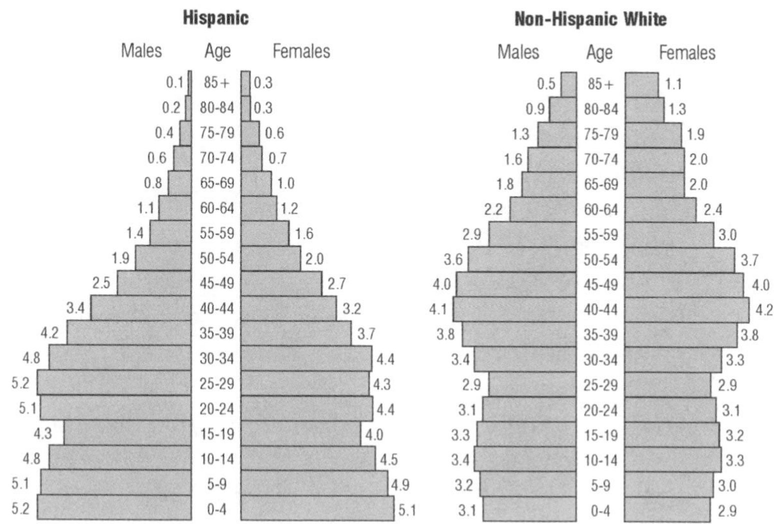

Figure 1-2. U.S. Population by Hispanic Origin, Age, and Sex, 2002
(Source: U.S. Census Bureau, 2002)

6. Of all foreign-born subgroups, Hispanic immigrants—especially those from Mexico—have the greatest need for the upward mobility that Adult Career Pathways would provide. Compared to immigrants from Europe and Asia, most of whom do about as well as our native population (some even better), Hispanic immigrants have lower levels of education and are more likely to be *underemployed.* And even among Hispanic immigrants as a whole, there are noticeable differences that seem to reflect native cultures. For example, among Hispanics age 25 or older living in the United States, Cubans, Puerto Ricans, and South Americans are more likely to

have graduated from high school than are Mexicans (U.S. Census Bureau, 2004). Compared to all other foreign-born groups, those from Mexico tend to lag in several areas.

(a) *Education*—Fewer than half of Mexican-born U.S. residents have high school diplomas (Camarota, 2001). The reasons don't always stem from a lack of educational aspirations. Many Hispanic immigrants have high educational aspirations, especially for their children, but those aspirations tend not to be realized (Immerwahr, 2003).

(b) *Skills*—Mexican immigrants are more likely to do menial labor that offers little opportunity for advancement. Most Hispanic immigrants work in nonprofessional service occupations such as building maintenance, food preparation and serving, and transportation and material moving (Kochbar, 2005). This trend may be due in part to cultural factors. Hispanics tend to settle in ethnic enclaves in which Spanish is the primary language and where communal attitudes may have a downward drag on occupational aspirations. Upon arriving in the United States, many Hispanics take low-paying jobs (a ready form of workforce entry) and never move on (U.S. Census Bureau, 2003). A recent study of college persistence among Hispanic students in automotive technology concluded that many Hispanics come to this country with a "laborer mentality" rather than a "college mentality." Many do not aspire to pursue high-level skills through postsecondary education because they do not picture themselves as college students (David, 2006).

(c) *Income* – Because of the employment situation described above, Mexican immigrants are more likely to live below the poverty line (Camarota, 2001).

(d) *Language*—As many as half of Hispanic adults living in the United States do not speak English. This severely limits their access to the educational opportunities necessary for upward mobility in the workplace (Pew-Kaiser, 2004; U.S. Census Bureau, 2003). Numerous community colleges and nonprofit groups offer ESL training, but the number is far from adequate (Wrigley et al., 2003).

Several federally funded programs provide employment, education, and training services that are either specifically for or are available to immigrants. In general, however, these programs are complex and fragmented (which may discourage participation by people with limited English skills) and far too limited in scope to meet growing need (Wrigley et al., 2003). Title I of the Workforce Investment Act (WIA) (U.S. Department of Labor) provides resources for "one-stop centers," which offer job search services and access to education and training. Title II of the WIA (also known as the Adult Education and Family Literacy Act) funds English language services, GED preparation, and other basic education services for adults who lack high school diplomas or basic literacy skills. The Refugee Resettlement Program (U.S. Department of Health and Human Services) helps nonprofit organizations and state resettlement offices provide ESL and job preparation services to recent arrivals. The Temporary Assistance for Needy Families (TANF) program provides block grants to states for cash assistance, employment and training programs, and related services for low-income families. The Pell Grant program of the Higher Education Act (HEA) provides educational funds that are available to legal immigrants.

In several respects, this target group overlaps the others described in this chapter. As stated above, a relatively high proportion of Hispanic students in American high schools do not graduate, and young Hispanics are much less likely than their white counterparts to earn college degrees (Garcia, 2002). Among reentering ex-offenders, approximately 21 percent are Hispanic (The Sentencing Project, n.d.). The U.S. Armed Services currently incorporate almost 70,000 foreign-born personnel, of whom a high proportion are from Latin America (Yau, 2005).

RETURNING VETERANS

In 1996 Congress established the Commission on Servicemembers and Veterans Transition Assistance in Title VII of the Veterans' Benefits Improvement Act of 1996 (Public Law 104-275). The Commission's report (CCSVTA, 1999), in addition to providing recommendations for updating the service and programs available (many of which dated from the end of World War II), provides many key facts that are relevant to this chapter. The following profile is based largely on that report, supplemented by information published by the Bureau of Labor Statistics (BLS) (2006) and other studies as noted.

Each year, the Department of Defense (DoD) "separates" approximately 238,000 servicemembers. Neither BLS nor DoD publishes demographic information pertaining specifically to that group on a year-by-year basis, but it provides relevant statistics for Gulf War-era veterans overall, along with statistics for veterans returning between 2002 and 2005.[2] We assume that the profile of the most recently returned servicemembers is comparable to that of the Gulf War-era veteran population as a whole, and especially the 2002–2005

Snapshot

Returning Veterans

How many? 238,000 a year

Ethnic makeup: Approximately mirrors the general population (except for Hispanics, who are more heavily represented in the general population)

Gender: 85% male, 15% female

Family status: 60% married; many have children

Educational status: Most have at least high school diplomas.

Services currently available: MGIB, Department of Veterans Affairs, Veterans' Employment and Training Service

Special problems: Many do not recognize the need for postsecondary education or have obligations that make pursuit of postsecondary education difficult.

Special needs: Depending on nature of service, technical and job-search skills

---

[2] The "Gulf War era" encompasses the years from 1990 to the present.

group. The following statistics and character traits reflect that assumption.

The ethnic makeup of the target group (2002–2005 returnees) is roughly as follows: 79 percent white, 16 percent African American, 7 percent Hispanic, and 1 percent Asian. Almost one in six returning servicemembers is now female.

The unemployment rates for the target group (by race and gender) are as follows: Overall, 11.9 percent; men, 9.9 percent; women, 28.5 percent; white, 9.3 percent; and African American, 28 percent. All of those figures are noticeably higher than the range of 4.6 to 6.3 percent for the general population during the same period (BLS). The CCSVTA report, which claims that the unemployment rates of newly separated veterans are even higher, blames the high unemployment rates on the failure of veterans' employment programs.

Unlike our other target groups, returning servicemembers have access to funds for college through the Montgomery GI Bill (MGIB). Yet, despite the availability of MGIB benefits, only about half of returnees take advantage of them (St. John & Tuttle, 2004). The reason may have more to do with *attitudes* toward college than *access* to college. Surveys have shown that college aspirations are not strongly associated with the desire to serve in the military. Most college-bound high school students look upon the military as a digression. As the CCSVTA report puts it, "increasing evidence indicates that high school graduates who are intent on obtaining a college education see military service as a detour away from their goal, rather than as a means of achieving it." A 1998 study based on the National Education Longitudinal Study of 1988 concluded that students in the "bottom income, top test score" group were the most strongly inclined to join the military (Akerhielm, Berger, Hooker, & Wise, 1998). Given that many of the young people who enlist in the military do not have college aspirations prior to enlistment, it should not be surprising that they do not seek postsecondary education following their discharge.

Returning veterans have strengths that other target groups often lack. They are disciplined, are more mature than nonveteran high school graduates, and (depending on the nature of their deployment) have a variety of technical skills.

EX-OFFENDERS

The last twenty-five years have witnessed a massive increase in incarceration in our country (Lynch & Sabol, 2001). As a result, policymakers and corrections experts have had to turn increasing attention to the problem of prisoner reentry. Reentry per se is not a new phenomenon, but the extent of reentry occurring today—more than 630,000 ex-offenders a year—far surpasses anything witnessed in the past, and the needs of those being released are greater (Petersilia, 2000). The release of large numbers of ex-offenders back into their communities—communities that in most cases contributed to the antisocial behavior that led to incarceration—also creates many collateral problems. Among the population of ex-offenders, problems such as child abuse, infectious disease, homelessness, unemployment, and domestic violence are common.

Many states find themselves caught up in a financial tug of war between the need for prison security and capacity and the need to

Snapshot

Ex-offenders

How many? Approx 630,000 returnees per year

Ethnic makeup: Much higher percentage of minority than in the general population

Gender: 93% male, 7% female

Family status: Many (esp. women) are parents of minor children.

Educational status: About half the total inmate population [approx 2,000,000] receives educational or vocational training (this percentage is decreasing); about 40% have neither HS diploma nor GED (% higher among minorities); young inmates less well educated than older inmates; men less well educated than women

Services currently available: In-house prerelease, educational, and vocational programs (but these have not kept pace with demand); nonprofit programs such as the Safer Foundation and RIO (Texas); federal programs such as FPI and PIE

Special problems: Wide variety of antisocial behaviors including substance abuse and gang-related activities; lack of technical and employability skills

Special needs: Counseling, occupational and academic education and training, substance abuse treatment (in many cases), wide range of social and family services (including housing and transportation)

prepare inmates for reentry. As they have increased their funding for prison construction and staffing, they have had to decrease funding for parole officers and education and rehabilitation programs. Fewer and fewer inmates receive the educational, occupational, and (in many cases) substance abuse help they need to reenter society with good prospects for avoiding recidivism. Because of in-prison gang activities, which are on the rise, many ex-offenders are more antisocial *after* release than they were before being incarcerated.

The population of ex-offenders is disproportionately minority and overwhelmingly male. (Only about 7 percent of current prison inmates are female.) Most come from, and return to, inner-city settings in which criminal behavior and incarceration are so common as to be considered normal, providing little incentive for ex-offenders to reform or for the next generation to avoid engaging in criminal behavior.

Among the greatest needs of ex-offenders are education and employment. Most leave prison with little education and training (many did not finish high school) and without prospects for employment. For many, steady work in gainful employment that is capable of supporting a family is an unfamiliar concept. The problem of poor employability skills among ex-offenders is compounded by the fact that many employers are reluctant to hire ex-offenders, and many states bar ex-offenders from employment in certain fields (Petersilia, 2000). Prerelease educational programs cover areas such as literacy skills, GED preparation, life skills, parenting, and employment training, but as the prison population continues to grow, educational resources have diminished (Goebel, 2005). Moreover, in choosing work assignments (which can include course taking), inmates often forego education in favor of higher-paying assignments.

Employment after release is strongly correlated to recidivism. Instability in employment leads to higher re-arrest rates, while steady employment and good wages tend to have the opposite effect. Research has also shown that when ex-offenders take advantage of opportunities to earn money by legitimate means, they are less prone to seek illegal means of obtaining money (Holzer et al., 2003; Solomon et al., 2004).

The federal government funds two programs designed to integrate work into the rehabilitative process: Federal Prison Industries (FPI) and Prison Industry Enhancement (PIE). The purpose of FPI (dating from 1934) is to offset the cost of incarceration. The program maximizes employment by focusing on low-wage jobs and therefore does not significantly improve participants' prospects for employment after release. PIE involves partnerships between private businesses and corrections facilities. Only a small number of inmates obtain employment through FPI or PIE. Beyond those programs, approximately half the state inmate population and almost all of the federal inmate population engages in some kind of work while incarcerated, but the work assignments often do not provide experiences that would be desirable to employers following release (Solomon et al., 2004).

Several independent organizations help ex-offenders find work. An excellent example is the Chicago-based Safer Foundation, which offers job counseling and placement, education in technical and employability skills training, and temporary housing. Over the past three decades, the foundation has helped several thousand ex-offenders find jobs. The Texas-based Re-Integration of Offenders Program (Project RIO) has also succeeded in reducing recidivism through employment, as has the Center for Employment Opportunities (CEO) in New York City. While these programs have made an impact, they do not represent the norm for ex-offenders. In general, "employment opportunities for former prisoners are few and far between" (Solomon et al., 2004).

REFERENCES

Adelman, C. (1998). The kiss of death? An alternative view of college remediation. *National Crosstalk.* National Center for Public Policy and Higher Education.

Akerhielm, K., Berger, J., Hooker, M., & Wise, D. (1998). *Factors related to college enrollment.* [Mathtech, Inc., Princeton, NJ]. Washington, D.C.: U.S. Department of Education (cited in St. John & Tuttle, 2004).

Aspen Institute. (2002). *Grow faster together. Or grow slowly apart. How will America work in the 21st century?* Author.

Balfanz, R., & Letgers, N. (2004). *Locating the dropout crisis: Which high schools produce the nation's dropouts? Where are they located? Who attends them?* Johns Hopkins University.

Barton, P. E. (2004). *Unfinished business: More measured approaches in standards-based reform.* Policy Information Report, Educational Testing Service.

Barton, P. E. (2005). *One-third of a nation: Rising dropout rates and declining opportunities.* Policy Information Report, Educational Testing Service.

Berkner, L., He, S., & Cataldi, E. F. (2002, December). *Descriptive summary of 1995–96 beginning postsecondary students: Six years later. Statistical analysis report.* National Center for Education Statistics, NCES 2003-151.

Bettinger, E. P., & Long, B. T. (2006). *Addressing the needs of under-prepared students in higher education: Does college remediation work?* National Bureau of Economic Research, Education Working Paper 11325.

Boesel, D., Alsalam, N., & Smith, T. M. (1998). *Research synthesis: Educational and labor market performance of GED recipients.* U.S. Department of Education.

Bridgeland, J. M., DiIluio, J. J., & Morison, K. B. (2006, March). *The silent epidemic: Perspectives of high school dropouts.* A report by Civic Enterprises in association with Peter D. Hart Research Associates for the Bill & Melinda Gates Foundation.

Bureau of Labor Statistics. (2006). *Employment situation of veterans summary.*

Camarota, S. (2001). Immigration from Mexico: Assessing the impact on the United States. Center for Immigration Studies.

Carey, K. (2004, May). *A matter of degrees: Improving graduation rates in four-year colleges and universities.* The Education Trust.

Carnevale, A. P., & Desrochers, D. M. (2002). *The missing middle: Aligning education and the knowledge economy.* Office of

Vocational and Adult Education, U.S. Department of Education.

Choy, S. (2002). *Nontraditional undergraduates: Findings from The Condition of Education 2002.* National Center for Education Statistics.

Clifton, D., & Nelson, P. (1995). *Soar with your strengths.* Dell.

Congressional Commission on Servicemembers and Veterans Transition Assistance. (1999). *Final report of the Congressional Commission on Servicemembers and Veterans Transition Assistance.* Author.

Crawford, M. (2001). *Teaching contextually: Research, rationale, and techniques for improving student motivation and achievement in mathematics and science.* Waco, Texas: CORD.

David. L. (2006). *Contributing factors to male Latino persistence and successful completion of the ESL component in a community college automotive program.* Diss., Argosy University-Schaumburg.

Day, J. C., & Newburger, E. C. (2002, July). *The big payoff: Educational attainment and synthetic estimates of work-life earnings.* U.S. Census Bureau, Current Population Report P23-210.

Friedman, T. (2005). *The world is flat: A brief history of the twenty-first century.* New York: Farrar, Straus and Giroux.

Garcia, P. (2002). *Understanding obstacles and barriers to Hispanic baccalaureates.* RAND Corporation and the Inter-University Program for Latino Research.

Goebel, K. (2005, August). Re-entry and corrections education. *Focus on Basics: Connecting Research & Practice,* 7(D), 9–10. National Center for the Study of Adult Learning and Literacy.

Greene, J. P., & Winters, M. A. (2006, April). *Leaving boys behind: Public high school graduation rates.* Civic Report no. 48. Center for Civic Innovation, Manhattan Institute.

Greico, E. (2003, October). *The foreign born from Mexico in the United States.* Migration Policy Institute.

Halperin, S. (1988a). *The forgotten half: Non-college youth in America.* William T. Grant Foundation Commission on Work, Family, and Citizenship.

Halperin, S. (1988b). *The forgotten half: Pathway to success for America's youth and young families.* William T. Grant Foundation Commission on Work, Family, and Citizenship.

Halperin, S. (1998). *The forgotten half revisited: American youth and young families, 1988–2008.* William T. Grant Foundation Commission on Work, Family, and Citizenship.

Harwell, S. H., & Blank, W. E. (2001). *Promising practices for contextual teaching.* Waco, Texas: CORD.

Hecker, D. E. (2001, November). Occupational employment projections to 2010. *Monthly Labor Review.*

Holzer, H. J., Raphael, S., & Stoll, M. A. (2003). *Employment barriers facing ex-offenders.* Urban Institute Roundtable: Employment Dimensions of Reentry—Understanding the Nexus between Prison Reentry and Work.

Immerwahr, J. (2003). *With diplomas in hand: Hispanic high school seniors talk about their future.* National Center for Public Policy and Higher Education, Public Agenda.

Jennings, J., & Rentner, D. S. (1998). Youth and school reform: From the forgotten half to the forgotten third. In S. Halperin (Ed.), *The Forgotten Half Revisited: American Youth and Young Families, 1988–2008* (pp. 83–99). William T. Grant Foundation Commission on Work, Family, and Citizenship.

Johnson, E. B. (2002). *Contextual teaching and learning: What it is and why it's here to stay.* Thousand Oaks, California: Corwin.

Kochbar, R. (2005). The occupational status and mobility of Hispanics. Pew Hispanic Center.

Lynch, J. P., & Sabol, W. J. (2001, September). *Prisoner reentry in perspective.* Crime Policy Report, Vol. 3. Urban Institute.

Martin, N., & Halperin, S. (2006). *Whatever it takes: How twelve communities are reconnecting out-of-school youth.* American Youth Policy Forum.

National Center for Public Policy and Higher Education. (2004). *Measuring up: The national report card on higher education, 2004.*

Orfield, G. (2004). Losing our future: Minority youth left out. In G. Orfield (Ed.), *Dropouts in America: Confronting the graduation rate crisis* (pp. 1–11). Cambridge, Mass.: Harvard.

Parnell, D. (2001). *Contextual teaching works! Increasing students' achievement.* Waco, Texas: CORD.

Petersilia, J. (2000, November). When prisoners return to the community: Political, economic, and social consequences. *Sentencing & Corrections Issues for the 21st Century: Papers from the Executive Sessions on Sentencing and Corrections,* no. 9.

Pew Hispanic Center and the Henry T. Kaiser Family Foundation. (2004, March). *Survey brief: Assimilation and language.* Author.

Phillippe, K. A., and Patton, M. (2000). *National profile of community colleges: Trends and statistics,* 3rd edition. Community College Press.

Rider University. (1998). *Who is most likely to succeed? New skills for a new workplace.* Rider University Center for the Development of Leadership Skills.

Schemo, D. J. (2006, September 2). At 2-year colleges, students eager but unprepared. *New York Times,* p. A1.

Sentencing Project, The. (n.d.). *Prisoners re-entering the community.* Author.

Solomon, A. L., Johnson, K. D., Travis, J., & McBride, E. C. (2004, October). *From prison to work: The employment dimensions of prisoner reentry.* Urban Institute Justice Policy Center.

St. John, E. P., & Tuttle, T. J. (2004). *Financial aid and postsecondary opportunity for nontraditional age, pre-college students.* The Education Resources Institute.

Wrigley, H. S., Richer, E., Martinson, K., Kubo, H., & Strawn, J. (2003, August). *The language of opportunity: Expanding employment prospects for adults with limited English skills.* The National Adult Education Professional Development Consortium and the Center for Law and Social Policy.

Yau, J. (2005). *The foreign born in the armed services.* Migration Policy Institute.

Our Vision

Components of the Adult Career Pathways Model

Dan Hull and Dick Hinckley

Every community and technical college in the United States receives applications from adult students in the six categories described in Chapter 1. Ideally those colleges would develop a unique program of study for each student. But, of course, that is impractical and cost-prohibitive. The typical (and largely ineffective) response to the needs of these students is threefold:

1. *Test the incoming students. If they show deficiencies in one or more academic areas, place them in remedial studies until they can "pass out."* Despite an annual cost of around a billion dollars, little is known about the effectiveness of remedial courses on a national level.[1] By adding to student requirements and extending the time needed to complete degree programs, in many cases their effects may actually be negative. As a result, many of the students

[1] E. P. Bettinger and B. T. Long, *Addressing the Needs of Under-Prepared Students in Higher Education: Does College Remediation Work?* (National Bureau of Economic Research, Education Working Paper 11325, 2006).

who take remedial courses in college never "pass out." They just "drop out."

2. *Once students have taken care of their remediation issues, advise them of conventional certificate or associate degree programs in which they can enroll, as either full- or part-time students.* Unfortunately, for many students, this isn't much help, if not supported by other measures. Nontraditional students (such as those under consideration in this book) tend to have personal obligations that make it extremely difficult for them to enroll in school, especially full-time. As a result, "nontraditional students are much more likely than traditional students to leave postsecondary education without a degree."[2]
3. *Provide short-term, "quick fix" vocational programs.* Many of the adults who apply to community colleges are able to receive some form of financial assistance that would allow them to attend the college full-time for one semester, or a 4–6-month period. Typically, these students are placed in "jump start" programs, where they are given "survival academics," personal needs assistance, entry-level skills training, and job-search skills. Most of these students leave the college after this initial period to take minimum-skills jobs. Frequently, they are employed for less than a year and are "back on the street," looking for more training or another job. This short-term strategy seldom produces long-term results.

In a few cases one or more of these three intervention efforts results in a successful transition for students, but it is the exception rather than the rule. In general, these approaches have drained college (and government) resources, contributed to nontraditional students' sense of failure, and done little to help employers who need world-class workers who can participate in company-based career ladder systems.

---

[2] S. Choy, *Nontraditional Undergraduates: Findings from* The Condition of Education 2002 (National Center for Education Statistics, 2002).

Our community and technical colleges didn't create this problem. On the contrary, they have worked hard to correct it. But the reality is that, in most instances, they have not been very successful. In their defense it should be pointed out that the development of a successful second-chance education strategy for adults has thus far confounded postsecondary educators because of the wide range of student abilities and personal needs involved, the lack of direction among people who most urgently need a second chance, and the difficulty those people face in accessing postsecondary education because of financial and personal limitations.

Most of the people in the six categories profiled in Chapter 1 are characterized by one or more (usually several) of the following traits:

1. Ages range from 18 to 50's (average: probably late 20's)
2. Must support themselves and, in many cases, minor dependents; cannot afford to be full-time students for 2–3 years; have limited access to financial aid
3. May need childcare and/or transportation
4. Academically weak; require remediation in reading, math, communication, and basic computer skills
5. May lack proficiency in English
6. Low self-esteem, confidence, and interest in academics
7. Lack study skills
8. Need "soft skills"
9. May not have concern for timeliness or quality of their work
10. Know about "the real world"; may have "survival skills" but do not know how to channel that knowledge into the acquisition of marketable career skills
11. Highly motivated to earn a decent wage
12. May be interested in careers but don't know how to pursue them
13. Have no career guidance

14. Average to above-average intelligence; most are probably very capable
15. Know very little about what it takes to obtain and keep family-supporting jobs

Based on the unique strengths and needs within each category of adults in need of "second chance" Career Pathways, it is possible to group the elements of an effective Career Pathway into seven components that constitute the ACP program as the authors envision it. Each phase, or "stage," of the curriculum addresses one or more of these components. (For the purposes of this paper, the term "stage" refers to a rung or step in the student's Career Pathway ladder.)

Descriptions of the seven components of the ACP model are provided in the following section. Figure 2-1 is intended to give a visual sense of how they interact and overlap in leading from unemployment (or underemployment) toward a common goal—employment in high-demand fields. The differences in shading in the figure are intended to suggest that some target groups will need some components more than others. The shading pattern would probably change from one target group to the next, or even from one individual to the next.

Component 1: Personal Needs

When they apply to colleges to gain career skills, the adults in our six categories usually require one or more forms of personal assistance. Most of these should be addressed in Stage 1. If personal needs are not identified and met early, adult students are often unable to enroll in school. Even those who do manage to enroll struggle to continue their studies long enough for them to be of any benefit. Most colleges have student intake staff, counselors, and financial aid officers who are dedicated to these tasks.

In planning for support of personal needs, both staff and students should understand that we are not talking about a short-term "quick fix." To be beneficial, an ACP will usually require an initial stage of approximately four months of full-time effort, followed by over three years of continuous studies on a part-time basis (six credit hours/stage). The need for support in meeting personal needs may be extensive during Stage 1 but should gradually diminish in subsequent stages. Ideally, the college will have partners who can assist in providing for these needs. Partners would include government programs, employers, faith-based organizations, and community service groups.

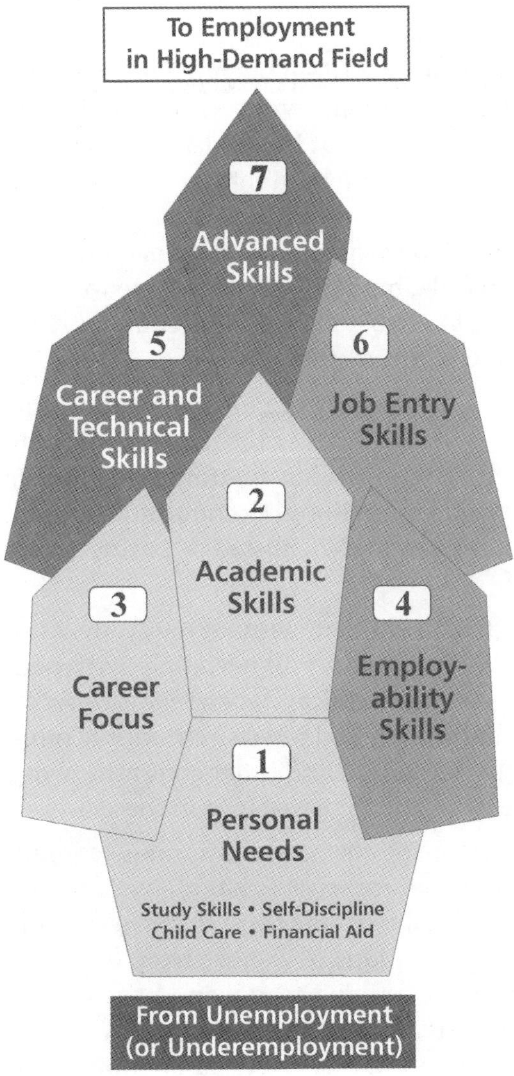

Figure 2-1. The Seven Components of an Adult Career Pathway

Personal needs can be grouped into four categories:

- *Financial*—Most adult students, particularly those who have been out of high school for five years or more, will not have enough financial resources to meet their educational expenses *and* provide for themselves and their dependents. The vast majority will require grants and/or student loans to pay these expenses during Stage 1 when they are full-time students.

  At the end of Stage 1 (Prep Stage), it is anticipated that successful ACP students will become employed by *participating employers,* at least on a part-time basis (30 hours/week), with paid release time and benefits, while they continue their education. We are proposing that, at the end of Stage 3, participating employers move their ACP students to full-time status but continue to provide paid release time to enable the students complete their educational requirements.

- *Logistical*—This category of personal need includes goods and services the students will need to participate in the ACP program. It includes childcare, transportation, and, in some cases, appropriate clothing. Community and faith-based organizations should be enlisted as partners to provide these services.

- *Personal*—It is likely that many of the students applying to enroll in ACP programs will need help with personal problems such as chemical dependency, self-discipline, learning disabilities, and job-search skills. Counselors and tutors from the college and other community organizations should be available for assistance in these areas.

  A significant factor encountered at many community colleges is the *cycle of poverty* that many of the adult students have experienced most of their lives. These students are the children of generations of welfare recipients, many of whom also dropped out of high school and have had only sporadic low-skilled jobs. Most of these applicants to the colleges have no family support (either financial or emotional) for committing to any form of continued education and career preparation. Mentors from the college staff must be available for one-on-one guidance, "hand holding," and "cheerleading" during Stage 1.

- *ESL*—Many first-generation immigrants from non-English-speaking countries struggle to communicate in English, particularly if they continue to live in homes and communities in which English is not the primary language. Their inability to read, understand, and speak English fluently is also a barrier to learning and can be a barrier to employment. ESL classes for this group are offered by colleges, community-based organizations, and faith-based organizations. We recommend that all students have at least basic English skills before they are admitted to Stage 1 (Prep Stage).

Component 2: Academic Skills

This component encompasses two types of skills:

- Remedial skills, i.e., the student proficiencies necessary to foundational work in postsecondary programs, and
- Career foundation skills, i.e., the math, communication, and science skills necessary to pursue careers in specific fields.

Remedial skills—Recent studies (e.g., by the Center for the Development of Leadership Skills at Rider University, 1998) have shown that employers value entry-level employees who possess useful academic skills (reading, writing, math) as much as they do career-specific skills. Unfortunately, most of the adults who apply to community and technical colleges score below the colleges' admission levels on mathematics, reading, and writing and require remediation to demonstrate adequate proficiency.

On average, colleges are less than 50 percent successful in correcting serious academic deficiencies in adult students (Adelman, 1998). We believe that the success rates can be improved significantly by using "contextual" strategies in teaching. Contextual teaching presents concepts in contexts that are familiar to students and that demonstrate the concepts' usefulness. Our experience at CORD has shown that most low academic achievers are concrete learners. That is, they learn best when abstract concepts are taught in the context of how they are used outside the classroom. When concrete learners are taught contextually, their achievement, confidence, and interest improve. There is no shortage of contextual teaching materials, but materials alone do not solve the problem. Contextualization of remedial math, science, and communication is unfamiliar to many teachers and thus requires professional development.[3]

Career foundations skills – Mathematics, science, and communication courses are also an important part of the career foundations curriculum, but they should be taught in the context of the career field that the student has chosen. Since 2001, extensive efforts have been made through Tech Prep practitioners in numerous states to foster collaboration among mathematics and career and technical education (CTE) faculty. These collaborations have resulted in the creation by CORD of authentic classroom problems in which students apply twenty-one essential math concepts to problems in fields such as construction, automotive service technology, business, IT, and agriculture.[4]

Component 3: Career Focus

Adults in our six target groups will most likely need career guidance just as much as teenagers in 4+2 Career Pathways do. The following elements of career guidance must be provided during Stage 1 the ACP:

- *Help students identify their strengths.* In their book *Soar With Your Strengths* (Dell, 1995), Don Clifton and Paula Nelson make the strong point that the way to develop your

---

[3] Contextual teaching is more than a remedy for low achievers. It is a proven strategy that helps all students achieve academic excellence. For more, see Michael Crawford, *Teaching Contextually: Research, Rationale, and Techniques for Improving Student Motivation and Achievement in Mathematics and Science* (CORD, 2001).

[4] Information on CORD's CTE math enrichment curriculum is available at www.cord.org.

abilities—and your self-esteem—is to identify your strengths and build on them. It seems that public education often tries too hard to make everyone a "well-rounded" person. Some students are naturally inclined to be "loners," and there are careers that require that type of personality. Helping students to identify their aptitudes and develop them in career pursuits can open doors of opportunity and improve self-image.

- *Help students identify where the good jobs are.* Counselors should be able to steer students in the direction of rewarding employment that will suit the students' interests over the long haul.
- *Help students choose educational pathways that will enable them to qualify for their careers of choice.* Students must be informed of realistic, available opportunities and the steps they must take to pursue them. One doesn't have to be a brain surgeon to enjoy a rewarding career in healthcare, if the costs and/or time commitments to learn brain surgery are unrealistic.
- *Help students acquire personal qualities and behaviors that will contribute to success in their chosen careers.*
- *Help students acquire strong job-search, application, and interview skills.*

Component 4: Employability Skills

The employability skills, or "soft skills," component of career and technical education has been identified, defined, and infused into the curriculum since it was introduced by SCANS in 1992. Employability skills are the third leg of the "standards stool" (academic, technical, employability). They include interpersonal relations, working in teams, critical thinking, and problem solving. In most 4+2 Career Pathways employability skills are infused into the curriculum and teaching strategies. In ACP, they must be redefined, expanded, and, in some instances, taught very early in the adult student's experience.

Many adults in our six targeted categories have very weak employability skills. Consequently, those skills—punctuality, quality of work, organization/neatness, organization rules, and teamwork—should be stressed during the Prep Stage of the ACP. Employability skills should also be reemphasized, required, and evaluated during every subsequent stage of the ACP, both at the college and in the workplace.

Today's workplace requires that employees be able to work in teams, think critically, and solve problems. Teamworking should be included in communication (language arts) courses and practiced in career and technical courses. Critical thinking and problem-solving skills are easily introduced into mathematics courses—if they are taught in the context of careers and technical skills—and can also be taught in communication and science courses. Every career and technical course should require and measure these skills.

Effective teaching and evaluation of employability skills require the participation of college and employer mentors. During Stage 1, college staff members should serve as mentors by helping and encouraging ACP students to learn, adopt, and practice employability skills in areas where the need for improvement is evident. This will probably require individual counseling sessions.

Employee mentors, if properly trained, can continue to reinforce these practices. It may seem that we are calling for an excessive amount of individual attention, support, and just plain "hand holding," but many adults in our six target areas are fragile and will need personalized help to overcome culturally entrenched attitudes and personal habits.

Component 5: Career and Technical Skills

Following the Prep Stage, students will be employed and will continue their studies part-time for several years. ACP curricula will prepare them for long-term careers, not just entry-level jobs.

The technical content of the curriculum for each ACP will be determined by a program advisory committee consisting of employers in the technical field addressed by the ACP. The committee will create (or modify) a skill standard that reflects anticipated employment opportunities in the relevant field. The curriculum content will be sequenced so that each stage of study corresponds to the knowledge and skills that the student-employee will need in the *next* step of his or her ACP. The student-employee should be formally acknowledged in some way at the completion of each stage of the curriculum.

Although the ACP student will have chosen a career field before taking career/technical education courses, he or she will not have been encouraged to focus on a particular job or level of attainment. Consequently, in the early stages of the curriculum, the career/technical component will concentrate on content that is applicable to a broad range of jobs within the student's chosen career field. The later stages of the curriculum will focus on knowledge and skills that pertain to specific jobs and the specialized requirements of particular employers.

The close relationship between academic (math, science, and communication) content and career/technical content was mentioned earlier. Because of this relationship, the teaching of both academic and career and technical courses should involve an infusion process that works in two directions. On the one hand, academic courses should be taught in the context of career problems. At the same time, a deliberate attempt should be made to infuse academic rigor into career and technical content and problem-solving exercises and practices.

It is likely that some aspects of the career and technical coursework can be learned, or applied, best "on the job." These areas of coordination between the college faculty and employers can be identified and facilitated by the program advisory committee.

Component 6: Job Entry Skills (including basic computer and Internet skills)

Job entry skills are skills necessary for employment after completion of the Prep Stage. These skills will, of necessity, be determined by the employers represented on the program advisory committee.

To have effective ACP programs that will lead to long-term employment and growth in careers, we will need to redefine "job entry skills." In the report *Who Is Most Likely to Succeed? New Skills for a New Workplace* (Rider University, 1998), a survey of

428 employers showed that they valued useful academics and soft skills as much or more than job-specific skills. The Rider University report also stressed the fluent use of computers and the Internet. Nearly all employers value workers who can use computers, productivity software, and/or the Internet. Basic IT skills are considered "job entry skills," and job applicants who have some proficiency in the organization's job-related applications of computers will have a distinct edge over applicants who do not.

Because today's workplaces call for broader skill sets than the workplaces of previous generations, every program advisory committee should call for a curriculum in the Prep Stage that is significantly different from the narrow job training we have been accustomed to seeing. For this to occur, leadership from participating employers must "come from the top," and the employer representatives in the program advisory committee must be at least "second-level managers" rather than "first-level supervisors" or job incumbents. Without buy-in from high-level management, employer organizations will not be able to participate at the level of commitment that the ACP program will demand.

This is critical to the success of the ACP program. The college CEO must be committed to this approach and be willing to seek an equally high level of commitment from the leadership of the participating employers.

Component 7: Advanced Skills

Advanced skills are a longer-range goal of the ACP. They will be introduced in only three or four of the later stages of the curriculum. Advanced (career) skills could be a place where "company-specific" knowledge or practices are taught. (This could be one way for an employer to hold on to the completers of the program.) Of course, some advanced skills could be taught at the employer workplace.

How an ACP partnership defines advanced skills will depend somewhat on the perceived goals of the program. If the program is designed to help the student acquire a certificate, and this is sufficient formal education to reach a desired rung on the career ladder, company-specific advanced skills are appropriate.

But if the goal is to enable the student to be a lifelong learner, and the program is designed to help the student obtain an associate degree (or higher), the advanced skills should be positioned so that the student can apply them toward higher education credits. In that situation, the credits would be considered "transferable." In an ideal scenario, advanced skills training would be dual purpose—it would satisfy company-specific skill requirements *and* move the student closer to long-term educational goals (for example, the final "2" of a 4+2+2 pathway). Developing that kind of scenario will require a high level of collaboration between business and education.

Putting the Components Together

Dan Hull

A Suggested Strategy and Curriculum Plan for Adult Career Pathways

Most of the strategies currently used by colleges to serve adults who are seeking career preparation are similar to the three plans cited in the previous chapter—*test and remediate, enroll in traditional plans,* or *provide short-term training for entry-level jobs.* These strategies are not yielding acceptable student retention and success rates, and they are not providing employers with sufficient numbers of capable, long-term employees who can progress through career ladders within an organization.

This problem is not going away. Studies show that successful student transitions from secondary to postsecondary are only beginning to improve. Secondary-postsecondary Career Pathways (as described in Hull et al., *Career Pathways: Education with a Purpose*) will certainly improve the transition rate over the next decade, but many adults and soon-to-be adults (many of whom are minorities and single mothers) need and deserve a realistic second-chance in education. And employers are already suffering from a lack of long-term, highly-skilled workers. Carnevale and Desrochers estimate that by 2020 baby boomers who retire will leave a void of over twelve million jobs unfilled by U.S. workers.[1]

It's time to think very differently about how we reeducate and prepare these adults. Yes, colleges have been "appointed" to lead this effort, but they cannot do it alone. A realistic, effective strategy will need the support and cooperation of employers and communities. Employer support must go beyond sitting on advisory committees and donating out-of-date equipment. Employers must be involved in making and executing plans, hiring adult students into the "corporate career ladder," and encouraging them to continue their education for several years. Community organizations, including faith-based organizations, must be willing to partner with businesses in meeting the personal needs of participating adults so that they can devote the time and concentration necessary for their "second chance" at education to succeed. Many suitable organizations already exist, but they tend to work in isolation. The time has come for a more comprehensive effort to pool resources and expertise in the accomplishment of common goals.

By 2020, baby boomers who retire will leave a void of over twelve million jobs unfilled by U.S. workers (Carnevale and Desrochers, 2002).

The following requirements are foundational to the design and delivery of the new curriculum:

1. Students must be able to commit to at least one semester or a 14–18-week period of full-time education. (For many adults, this is not realistic without financial support, for both school expenses and personal needs.)
2. Students must have access to part-time (at least half-time) jobs following the Prep Stage.

---

[1] A. P. Carnevale and D. M. Desrochers, *The Missing Middle: Aligning Education and the Knowledge Economy* (U.S. Department of Education, 2002).

3. Employers in the same fields (e.g., telecommunication, construction, manufacturing), who might normally think of themselves as competitors, must be willing to work together in supporting the program, especially by hiring students—**part-time only**—after the Prep Stage.
4. Employers in similar fields must be willing to commit to a common "career ladder" in which each student is promoted, given a raise, and/or publicly commended each time he or she completes a stage of education/training.
5. Curriculum should integrate the essential components identified in Figure 2-1 in each 4–6-month period of the curriculum.
6. Programs must provide frequent rewards so that students can mark their progress and see "light at the end of the tunnel."

A Ladder Curriculum that Correlates to a Career Ladder

The term "ladder curriculum" is not new. It is frequently used in healthcare programs to describe multitiered sequences of courses in which each tier, or group of tiers, correlates to a level of progression in an employment "career ladder." In nearly all cases, a ladder curriculum and a career ladder are used where there are "job certifications," such as in nursing and other fields within healthcare. Some apprenticeship programs also employ a modified approach to a ladder curriculum matched to a career ladder.

We are proposing that ACP programs adopt a ladder curriculum/career ladder strategy that can be applied to almost any career field. To accomplish this will require close cooperation between colleges and employers in relevant career fields or career clusters. In a sense, the work of the college/employer committee would be to create a series of informal job certifications that could be tied to blocks of the curriculum. A graphical representation of the ladder curriculum/career ladder is shown in Figure 3-1.

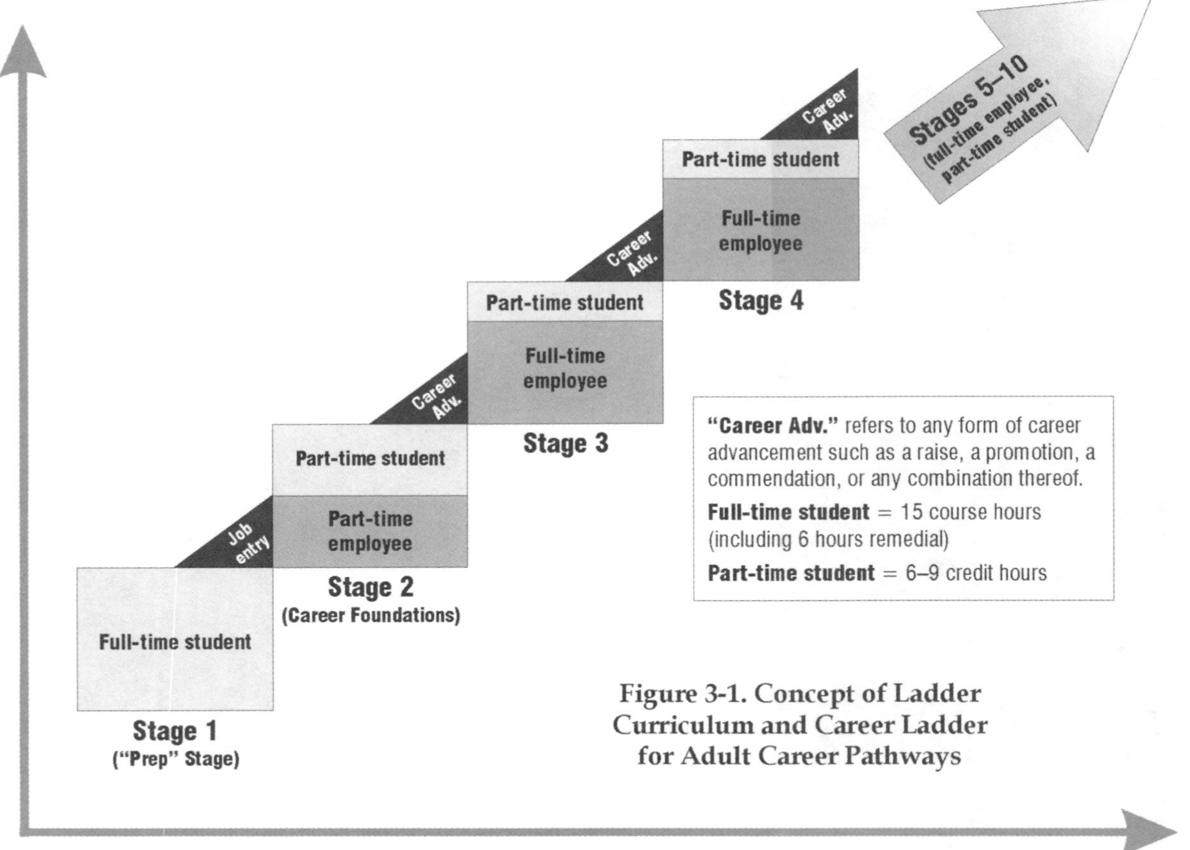

Figure 3-1. Concept of Ladder Curriculum and Career Ladder for Adult Career Pathways

Stage 1 (the Prep Stage) is typically a time when adults are given the opportunity to attend as full-time students. They will generally need parts of six of the curriculum components:

1. Personal needs
2. Academic skills (including effective remediation)
3. Career focus
4. Employability skills
5. Career and technical skills
6. Job entry skills (including basic computer and Internet skills)

Most of the first stage coursework will be recognized as "nontransferable credits." It is a period for "repositioning" these adults to acquire the confidence, career focus, discipline, academic foundation, and employability skills that demonstrate their potential to enter higher education and long-term employment. As a decisive first step, the "prep stage" also serves as an opportunity for students to show employers that they have the interest and potential to reach long-term goals. Hopefully, at the end of this stage the students will be hired (by participating employers) at the bottom rung of a career ladder. In a typical situation, the student would work part-time (~30 hours/week) and continue his or her education in the ladder curriculum.

Employers who hire these adults are "betting on their future." These adults are not limited to typical "job skills." They have broad skills that, hopefully, demonstrate the potential to grow in knowledge, experience, and value to their employers.

In Stage 2, most students will need to work 20–30 hours/week to provide support for themselves and their dependents. They will continue to require some outside support for personal needs such as childcare and finances. Their course load should average nine credit hours, mostly in academics and career and technical subjects. Employers will participate in the students' education by deliberately engaging the students in tasks that require "soft skills." These student/employees will be assigned employee mentors, who will assist them in adjusting to the environment of the job and help them with personal and academic needs. Students who complete the second stage and perform satisfactorily on the job will be recognized by their employers with certifications, job promotions, salary increases, and/or full-time job status.

In Stage 3, most students are full-time employees who take at least six credit hours in the ladder curriculum. Some employers may be able to provide paid leave at the end of the work day to allow the students to attend classes. Coursework will cover both academic (*in-context*) and career and technical subjects. Upon successful completion of the coursework and satisfactory performance on the job, students will again be recognized with an increase in status and/or salary or in some other form.

At about the third stage (and beyond), employers may be tempted to lure students away from school to take on full-time jobs and narrow, company-specific training. The authors see this as short-sighted and counterproductive for both the employer and the student. Employers are strongly encouraged to help students complete their programs of study and position themselves for even further education—even if, in so doing, the employers risk losing workers to competitors.

In Stage 4, coursework will almost be entirely career-related. A minimum of six credit hours should be taken. Hopefully, the employer will recognize the long-term value of the student/employee and reimburse the student/employee's educational expenses. This should reduce the amount of outside personal support required. Upon successful completion of the coursework and satisfactory work performance, students/employees are again recognized with an increase in job responsibilities and compensation.

In Stages 5 and 6, the curriculum begins to include advanced skills that are not only earning postsecondary credit but are also becoming more specific to the needs of the employer organization. Again, satisfactory work performance and completion of the assigned coursework will earn additional job credentials and compensation.

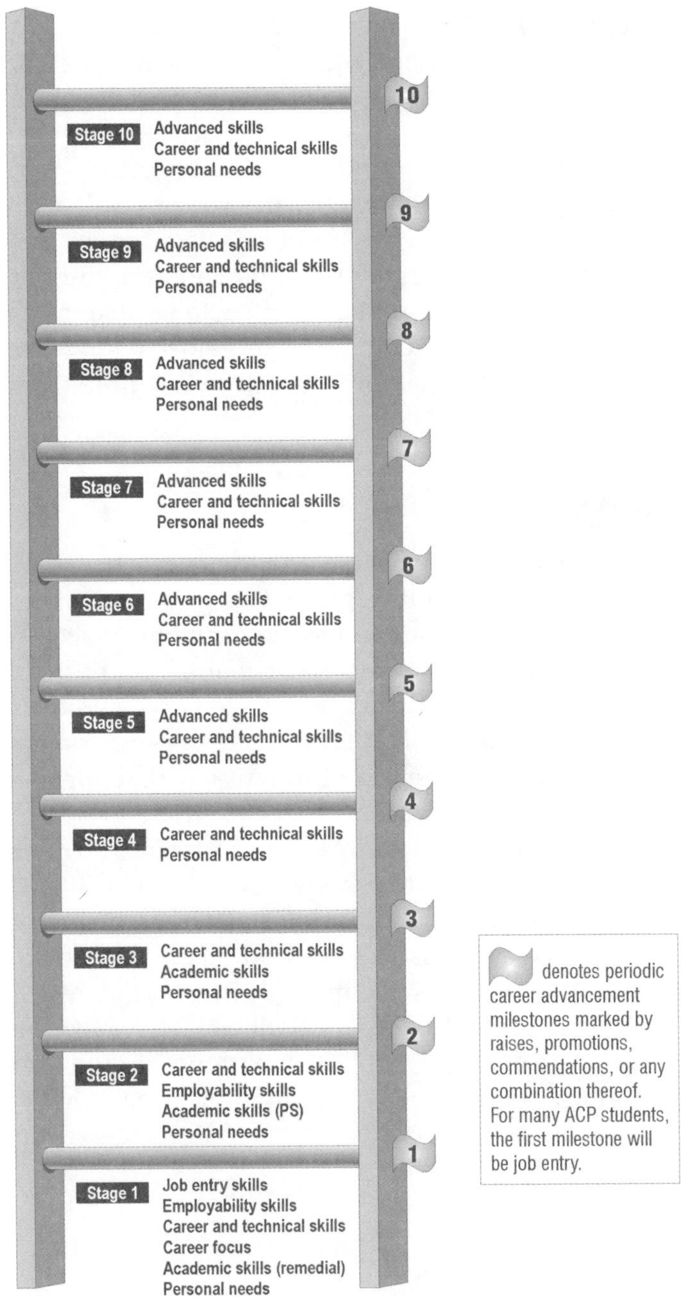

Figure 3-2. Model Ten-Stage Ladder Curriculum for Adult Career Pathways

In Stages 7–10, the student should complete the requirements for an associate degree or certificate. The course content in this stage (or stages) will be more directly job-related. Completion of this curriculum and the associated work experience will establish a foundation for a lifelong career and further education and/or training as desired or needed. This prescribed phase of an ACP will be completed, but the door to career opportunities and higher education and training is just beginning to open. The student can expect to be able to achieve a desirable lifestyle, and the employer has gained a long-term employee with the potential for future growth within the organization.

THE CHALLENGE

In the first three chapters we have provided evidence that undereducated young adults represent a significant challenge to our community colleges, our employers, and our society. But even more importantly, they represent a failure of our public education system to provide to every citizen of our country the opportunity to participate in interesting, rewarding careers. This missed opportunity also represents many jobs that our employers will have to export to other countries.

Short-term strategies to address this problem are largely ineffective because they only produce short-term results. The workplace is constantly changing. Job skills can quickly become obsolete. To survive in today's world, adults need the broad skills necessary to progress and grow throughout their working years. To be lifelong *earners,* we must all be lifelong *learners.*

Giving career-limited adults a meaningful "second chance" in education will require a new and different approach.

The ladder curriculum/career ladder strategy proposed in this book is not entirely new or untested, but its use has been limited to careers that are highly regulated and certified. We are suggesting that this strategy be adopted in the many fields that are not regulated or certified. But, to accomplish this, groups of local employers with common job needs will have to create an *informal certification process*. In the last 5–8 years, career and technical education has moved much closer to being *standards-based*. As a result, the process for designing and implementing a career ladder curriculum is fairly well understood.

Short-term strategies to address this problem are largely ineffective because they only produce short-term results. The workplace is constantly changing. Job skills can quickly become obsolete. To survive in today's world, adults need the broad skills necessary to progress and grow throughout their working years. To be lifelong *earners*, we must all be lifelong *learners*.

Furthermore, the progress made among academic and technical educators to improve student success for these *applied learners* provides reasonable assurance that such a curriculum is achievable with these adult students.

The greatest challenge will not be the curriculum or the student achievement. It will be finding realistic answers and solutions to the following questions:

1. **Will employers be willing to make the necessary investment in human capital?** The proposed plan will require that local employers hire ACP students after they have completed the first stage of the curriculum, and support their continuing educational pursuit for three years, by providing mentoring, recognition/rewards, paid release time, and reimbursement for educational expenses. This is expensive, but the payoff for this type of investment is that the participating employers will have gained long-term employees who can grow in their organizations and help the organizations to prosper. The consequence of not making this investment is that the need for highly skilled workers will continue to grow, as

will the population of underemployed (or unemployed) adults who are qualified only for low-wage jobs. For employers, it really boils down to a choice between paying now and paying later. Employer participation must be supported by commitment at the highest level in the organization.

2. **Will employers who normally would compete with one another for highly skilled workers be willing to cooperate for the sake of workforce development in their communities?** If the ACP process is to work, employers who adopt similar career ladders for their ACP students/employees must agree not to "raid" one another's students/employees while they are in the 3-year ACP program. They must be willing to take the risk that when employees complete their ACP programs, they may elect to "jump ship" (get jobs with other employers who lure them away for a little more money). The participating employers must be willing to provide incentives that are sufficient to earn company loyalty.
3. **Will local employers, college administrators, and state and regional funding and accreditation groups agree on a common curriculum for the ACP that will match their career ladders?** If local employers insist that the advanced courses on the last four stages be specifically aligned with their companies' peculiar needs, the credits earned for those courses might not be counted toward AS degrees or be transferable to other institutions. (That is, the pathway will be considered *terminal*.) And a college that provides courses that earn only nontransferable credits might not receive full compensation from its state funding agency. These are trade-offs that must be fully explored and agreed upon.
4. **Will there be sufficient unity, flexibility, and cooperation among colleges, employers, states, and community-based organizations to provide for the personal needs of these adult students until they can "learn enough to earn enough"?** Financial and personal aid for most of the students in ACP programs is usually

available somewhere in the community. But can it be accessed, organized, prioritized, and accumulated to adequately support these students? The supplying of personal needs for ACP students can simplistically be viewed in two phases:

- **In Stage 1,** financial assistance and educational assistance would be funneled to the student from the college (which may receive funds from state allocations, grants, and other sources). Other personal needs may be provided by the college and community/faith-based organizations.
- **In the remaining stages** (after the student is employed), most financial and educational expenses will be borne by the student and the employer. Other personal needs (such as childcare and transportation) should continue to be provided by community/faith-based organizations, until the student/employee is sufficiently independent to provide for these personally.

The leadership and vision necessary to make this plan succeed must come from employers, educators, community leaders, and policymakers at the very highest levels.

It's a huge challenge, but we think it's doable—and that it must be done.

Chapter 4 Preview

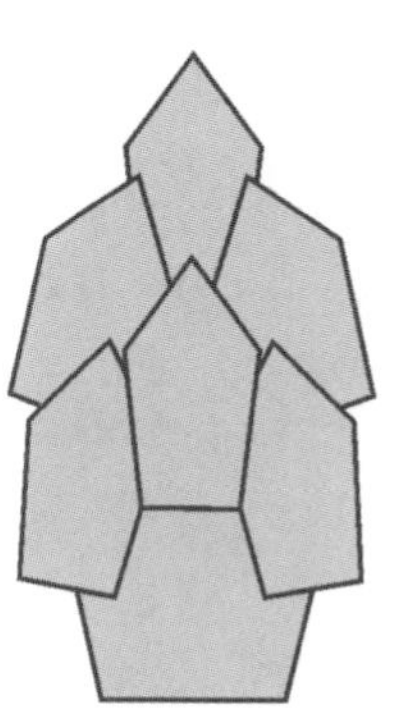

There are many good, hard working leaders in colleges, communities, and the private sector who are successful at modifying and replicating practices that were developed and modeled somewhere else. To our knowledge, the ACP vision, as we have outlined it, does not have a complete working model, although there are successful practices of individual elements. We are calling for a new initiative; thus, leadership to create and sustain ACP programs will need to come from the highest levels of leadership in our colleges, communities, and businesses. We suggest that the partnership be put together by the college president. Details about the ACP partnership and suggestions for the steps in its formation are included in this chapter.

DH & RH

Putting the Partnership Together

Dick Hinckley

If this nation is to continue to compete in an increasingly competitive global economy, it must make the most of its human capital. The career-limited population groups identified in Chapter 1 represent a large, diverse, and potentially productive resource that we cannot afford to neglect. Yet the reality is that we *are* neglecting many.

The previous chapter posed a challenge, stated in the form of four questions:

1. Will employers be willing to make the necessary investment in human capital?
2. Will employers who normally would compete with one another for highly skilled workers be willing to cooperate for the sake of workforce development in their communities?
3. Will local employers, college administrators, and state and regional funding and accreditation groups agree on a common curriculum for the ACP that will match their career ladders?
4. Will there be sufficient unity, flexibility, and cooperation among colleges, employers, states, and community-based

organizations to provide for the personal needs of these adult students until they can "learn enough to earn enough"?

If ACP programs are to become a widespread reality, the answer to all of those questions must be a resounding ***yes***. But that's a tall order. How do we get there? Schools and businesses and government agencies all have their own agendas, sometimes complementary, more often not. In the case of businesses, many are in direct competition. The answer is *leadership*. Meeting the ACP challenge will require strong, committed leadership, community by community.

One of the major premises of this book is that, for the most part, the leaders are already out there. Most communities already have the educational, political, and business leaders necessary to make ACP programs a reality. The question is whether those leaders will be willing to come together in pursuit of a common goal—a goal that has the potential to elevate the quality of life in their communities, but one that will also require giving up some of their fiercely guarded turf.

Positive steps are being taken all across the country. It is possible to identify many partnerships in which educators, business leaders, and community policymakers have produced success stories. The catalyst for those programs is usually some kind of government program that provides funding. But the driving force is always local leadership. Without strong leaders, the vast majority of government-funded programs fizzle out as soon as the funding stops.

WHO SHOULD PARTICIPATE? THE FOUR "LEGS" OF ACP SUPPORT

ACP programs require a systematic, communitywide approach in which key leaders come together with a shared purpose. There's no limit on where those leaders can come from. But, at a minimum, four groups of people must be well represented:

- Employers
- Postsecondary educators

- Community leaders
- High-level policymakers

Working together, those groups can support ACP programs like the legs of a four-legged footstool. Consider that image for a moment—a simple, four-legged wooden footstool. As long as the four legs are of equal length and firmly attached, the stool is extremely durable and can support considerable weight. But if one of the legs is too short, or is removed altogether, the stool topples. ACP programs are a little like that stool. As long as they enjoy the support of the four groups described in this section, they can keep going strong, regardless of changes in the economy or federal policies.

Let's look at each of the four ACP "legs" in a little more detail.

Leg 1: Employers

Employer involvement is essential to the success of ACP programs.

The ACP concept presented in this book calls upon employers to invest both money and expertise in the support and education of ACP student-employees. As stated in Chapter 3, Stage 1 of the ACP ladder involves full-time coursework. For most ACP students, this means that for one full semester they will need a significant amount of help in meeting their normal financial obligations. While ACP coordinators will be able to obtain some of the necessary financial assistance from nonprofit sources, businesses must also do their part. And they should be willing to do so. Over time, ACP student-employees will be able to repay their employers' investment several times over in the form of long-term service and high-quality workmanship.

The other area in which employer involvement is essential is expertise, especially expertise pertaining to the clusters they represent. Employers are uniquely qualified to say what their employees should know and be able to do. If they expect the graduates of the technical programs in their localities to have the right skills, they must tell educators what those skills are. One of the biggest complaints of employers all across the country is that they can't find qualified workers. ACP programs give them an opportunity to have a voice in how and what their future employees are taught.

As to specifically which employers should be involved, that will depend on the clusters being addressed in any given setting. Any mid-size-to-large community will have a fairly substantial number of adults who are either unemployed or underemployed. Collectively that group will represent a broad range of interests and aptitudes. Ideally, the community would put in place a *range* of ACP programs that is broad enough to serve all of those people. But of course that is not possible. A more realistic approach is to begin with a single cluster represented by *local* employers. If the resulting, narrowly focused, ACP program is a success, it not only will fulfill its primary mission—improving the lives of its student participants and giving its employer partners access to highly qualified workers—but will serve as a model for other programs.

Employer representation has both horizontal and vertical aspects. It is horizontal in the sense that, if the community has several businesses in the same cluster, they should *all* be represented, even if they are competitors. Employer representation is vertical in the sense that, for any given business, at least three levels of activity should be reflected: executive, middle management, and frontline production. This is not to say that frontline workers should serve on ACP advisory committees. But certainly their point of view should be well represented. And when we use the term *executive*, we are referring to the highest echelons in the company. The participation of CEOs is critical to the successful implementation of ACP.

Leg 2: Educators

The educational focus of ACP programs will be primarily at the two-year postsecondary level. This is because, on the whole, community and technical colleges have the programs and personnel necessary to teach the skills needed by ACP student-employees. Also, because of the average socioeconomic level of their students, two-year colleges often provide social services—

childcare, for example—that many ACP students will require, especially during Stage 1.

The ACP concept does not ask that community and technical colleges do anything radically different from what they are already doing. But it does ask that they be willing to bend a little in tailoring their programs to the specific needs of local employers. Many college personnel will balk at this idea. Part of the colleges' job, they would say (truthfully), is to maintain certain standards, which is difficult even under the best of circumstances. Community college faculty members are keenly aware of the constant downward drag on the standards they work hard to enforce. Some teachers, especially among those in academic areas, will view ACP ladder curricula as "watered down." They will also resist the idea of giving college credit for employer-specific training. The key to bringing community and technical college personnel on board is to emphasize the commonality between their goals and the needs of the employers for whom their graduates will eventually go to work. Both spheres—education and business—seek an environment in which people are well-equipped to work for the local companies who need their services.

In the previous section, we noted that employer partners must be represented at the highest level—the CEO. The same applies to colleges. If ACP programs are to succeed, they must have the support and direct involvement of college presidents and chancellors. Those people have the authority to make things happen in their institutions, and they are usually well connected in their communities and, thus, can bring other key people to the table.

Leg 3: Community Leaders

This group includes public servants such as mayors, city council members, city managers, and county-level policymakers. It also includes leaders of private entities such as nonprofit foundations and faith-based organizations. In this chapter we will focus more on public officials. (Private charitable and faith-based organizations are discussed more fully in Chapter 12.)

Community leaders possess three things that make them indispensable to ACP programs: authority, visibility, and connections.

- *Authority*—Every public official has some level of authority that enables him or her to carry out an agenda. When ACP programs become an item on that agenda, things happen. The key is *sustained* commitment. If a city mayor, for example, were to make ACP programs a consistent theme in his or her administration, sooner or later that commitment would produce tangible results.
- *Visibility*—Public officials, especially the highest ranking in the community, are well known. That means that when they speak, people listen. Even something as simple as an editorial in the local newspaper will get the attention of influential people in the community. Most public officials also have the ability to focus local media attention. When the mayor invites a local television network to cover an event—the unveiling of a fledgling ACP program, for example—chances are good that a camera crew and reporter will be there. On a local level, public officials have a strong voice in determining what events are newsworthy.
- *Connections*—Public officials know prominent people in the community. That alone makes them indispensable in the support of ACP programs. ACP programs are all about bringing people together in common cause. Public officials, many of whom are well-established businesspeople, have the influence and connections necessary to make that happen.

Leg 4: Policymakers

In this context, we are using the term *policymaker* broadly to refer to any person who establishes policy, whether an employer, an educator, or a community leader. Obviously, then, this would include state and federal elected officials and appointed heads of agencies at those levels. We also include accrediting and certification bodies associated with employer groups, industry clusters, and colleges. Their support is considered essential because they set the standards that ACP programs must meet, and they establish the credibility of the education and training that ACP programs provide.

WHY SHOULD THE "LEGS" WANT TO PARTICIPATE?

In the preceding section we answered a question—"Who should participate?" Our answer consisted of four groups, which we compared to the legs of a footstool. In this section we must tackle an equally important question: "Why should the 'legs' want to participate at all?" That question is important for one simple reason: If the "legs" don't *want* to participate, they won't. Most of the people whose support is urgently needed have never heard of ACP, and many people look down on any form of "vocational" education. (In fact, ACP programs will not provide narrow "vocational" education, but that doesn't change the perception.) Consequently, "putting the partnerships together" (to return to the title of our chapter) will require the ability to persuade the "legs" to see the benefits of ACP programs, not just to the less fortunate in their communities, but to themselves.

Following are five reasons the "legs" should want to participate.

1. *ACP programs will help to alleviate the critical worker shortages faced by American businesses and industries*—The United States faces critical worker shortages in virtually every employment field. This is one of the main reasons so many U.S. companies have relocated offshore. And it's not just low-wage jobs that are going vacant; it's high-skill, high-wage jobs in manufacturing, services, construction, logistics, and financial services. To date, this trend has not leveled off. It is increasing at an alarming rate.
2. *ACP programs give unemployed and underemployed adults the opportunity to succeed in well-paying jobs, thereby helping both themselves and their communities*—Many studies have shown a positive correlation between unemployment and social ills such as crime, domestic violence, child abuse, and substance abuse. Every community leader

should look favorably on programs that place rewarding employment within the reach of people who have struggled to rise above the poverty line.

3. *By increasing the availability of well-trained workers, ACP programs make communities more attractive to new businesses*—Businesses look carefully before moving to new locations. They want to know about property values, utilities, taxes, schools, access to major thoroughfares and airports, and—perhaps most important of all—whether they will be able to find qualified employees in adequate numbers. In fact, one of the primary functions of every chamber of commerce is to market its community as a place where new businesses can thrive. ACP programs have the potential to enhance community image by increasing *local* supplies of capable, well-trained workers.
4. *ACP programs can reduce the cost to communities of unemployment and social services*—Unemployed persons are consumers of public dollars and services. Putting those persons to work has a positive effect on the use of tax dollars.
5. *By increasing employment, ACP programs can increase tax revenues, thereby helping to fund public services and infrastructure*—Employment taxes and the expenditure of disposable income on goods and services enable communities to build libraries, maintain roads, support the arts, and provide other services that promote the general welfare.

Ultimately, ACP programs give communities a highly trained and motivated workforce, productive citizens, and a sense of assurance as they move forward into the future. When representatives of our four support legs—employers, educators, community leaders, and policymakers—are asked to support ACP programs, they are not being asked merely to help the less fortunate in their communities. They are being asked to make an investment in their communities that will also bring real benefits to themselves and their constituents. Figure 4-1 summarizes those benefits.

What Are the Benefits?

To Employers

- Increased worker productivity
- Entry-level workers who have good technical and employability skills and thus require only minimal on-the-job training, if any
- Access to adequate *numbers* of qualified workers
- Workers who have the necessary basic skills in reading, writing, and communication
- Workers with positive attitudes, who see learning as a lifelong process and are open to new opportunities to learn
- Workers who are loyal to their employers

To Educators

- Increased knowledge of what their students should learn in order to be competent in their fields
- An increased source of students for their programs (One of the goals of ACP programs will be to bring people to the colleges who would not otherwise venture there. This is discussed more fully in Chapter 12.)
- Clear career pathways for use in counseling students
- Enlarged opportunities for student internships
- Greater job placement rates for their programs
- Access to improved laboratory equipment through partnerships

To Community Leaders

- Improved employment rates of citizens
- Greater alignment of community resources
- Increased income levels in the community
- Improved economic development opportunities
- Strengthened business environment
- Reduced poverty levels, crime rates, and need for extraordinary human services

To Policymakers

- Increased impact of funded programs and services
- Improved outcomes of social policy

Figure 4-1. Benefits of ACP Programs to the People Who Support Them

WHAT MUST ACP SUPPORTERS BE WILLING TO GIVE—AND GIVE UP—TO PARTICIPATE?

Obviously, supporting ACP programs will require *giving*—of time, effort, influence, and (sometimes) money. For some people, that will involve real sacrifice. But the greatest challenge to potential ACP supporters is not so much what they must be willing to give, but what they must be willing to *give up*. In most cases, the things given up will be only fears and misperceptions, but fears and misperceptions die hard. For example, employer partners will have to be willing to work with, not against, their competitors. In the business world, that's counterintuitive. Survival in business involves maintaining a competitive edge. Some potential employer partners will fear that, in giving money to ACP programs, they risk losing their investment twice over. If an ACP student in whom an employer has invested goes to work for a competitor, not only is the supporting employer's investment lost, the competitor now enjoys the value added by the skills acquired via the ACP program. Worse still, the former employee may reveal trade secrets to the competitor. While those fears are not irrational, we believe that they will be realized only rarely. The ACP concept presented in this book is based on the assumption that an employer's investment in an ACP student will foster employee loyalty, and that very few ACP program completers will "jump ship."

Educators must likewise be willing to give up certain fears and misperceptions. For example, many educators are disdainful of any form of job training and will initially resist any attempt to bring industry personnel into the educational process. They believe (erroneously) that contextual teaching—which stresses hands-on applications and the usefulness of information—is inferior to conventional, abstract teaching and is suitable only for low-achieving students. That is a misperception. Contextual teaching can be as high-level as teachers choose to make it, and all students gain in motivation and sense of purpose when they see how information is used outside the classroom. (For more on contextual teaching, see Chapter 7.)

Fortunately, some of what ACP supporters must be willing to give up will be given up easily. For example, community colleges all across the country have spent millions of dollars setting up sophisticated technical programs but struggle to enroll enough students to keep the programs going. No educator would resist the prospect of having to give up low enrollment and the constant struggle to recruit students. Similarly, employers will welcome the prospect of having to give up the high cost of employee turnover and the friction that often exists between management and labor.

So, what will ACP program supporters have to give up? Mainly isolation, failure, and uncertainty of the future. Figure 4-2 presents a summary.

What Must Be Given Up?

By Employers

- Fear that, by partnering with competitors, they will give away trade secrets
- Fear that the students in whom they invest will "jump ship," causing loss of investment and giving competitive advantage to competitors
- High employee turnover and retraining costs
- Ill will between management and labor

By Educators

- Believing that partnering with business and industry somehow dilutes their curriculum
- Misperception that education and career preparation are antithetical
- Misunderstanding of contextual teaching and applied academics
- Low enrollment; recruitment hassles

By Community Leaders

- High unemployment in their communities
- Lack of coordination among human services efforts

By Policymakers

- Continuation of programs and services that perpetuate rather than solve the social ills created by unemployment and poverty

Figure 4-2. What ACP Supporters Must Be Willing to Give Up

TAKING OWNERSHIP: THE SPECIAL ROLE OF COMMUNITY AND TECHNICAL COLLEGE PRESIDENTS

Now that we have identified the four "legs" of ACP support, and what they have to both gain and lose by becoming involved, we should consider who takes the first steps. Just as every chemical reaction depends on a catalyst, the formation of successful ACP programs will depend on human catalysts—people who take ownership of the ACP concept in their communities and do whatever it takes to get, and keep, the process going. While human catalysts can emerge from any of the four "legs," we believe that chancellors and presidents of local community and technical colleges are best suited to that role.

Virtually every square mile of the United States is served by a community or technical college. With more than 1200 campuses nationwide, not to mention many hundreds more of satellites and outreach centers, the U.S. system of community and technical colleges constitutes the single most potent workforce development network in the country. Most community and technical colleges consider accessible, low-cost workforce development programs their primary mission. In fulfilling that mission, they seek benefits to both the students who pass through their doors and the area employers for whom those students will eventually work. In other words, their mission and the mission of ACP programs are essentially one and the same.

Just as every chemical reaction depends on a catalyst, the formation of successful ACP programs will depend on human catalysts—people who take ownership of the ACP concept in their communities and do whatever it takes to get, and keep, the process going.

Another reason community and technical college presidents should take the lead in forming ACP partnerships is that community and technical colleges are generally viewed as neutral entities that stay out of local politics and business competition. Community college presidents typically have good working relationships with people on "both sides of the aisle" and seek the overall betterment of their service areas. They are able to take a long-term view and carry out nonpartisan agendas accordingly.

Community and technical colleges are already the default providers of services and programs that most ACP students would need. In other words, those colleges are already doing much of what the ACP concept calls for. For them, the transition to full-fledged ACP programs would involve mainly a new level of collaboration with business, designation of an ACP coordinator (see following paragraph), a new emphasis on contextual teaching, and a willingness to tailor their programs to the specific needs of area employers. If community and technical college presidents are willing to take ownership of ACP programs and are committed to making the necessary adjustments, the potential benefits of ACP will become a reality.

Designating the ACP Coordinator—Early in the process of forming an ACP partnership, the college CEO should name a member of the college staff to be the ACP coordinator. (Ultimately, this person may have a rank in the college similar to a dean.) In the formative stages, the ACP coordinator will be responsible for data gathering, meeting logistics, reports, publicity and other forms of communication. As the ACP program becomes a reality, the ACP coordinator will become the responsible manager of the organization and development/operation process, hiring staff, convening *second-level* meetings of faculty and employer representatives, building relationships with appropriate community leaders and searching for sources of state and federal funding.

CREATING A SENSE OF URGENCY

Bringing community leaders together to accomplish a common purpose is difficult, even under the best of circumstances. It's hard to get people's attention unless they perceive that the situation at hand affects them in a personal way. On the other hand, when communities realize that they face a serious common threat, they are able to accomplish remarkable feats of collective will. We all witnessed this in New York City in September of 2001. One of the main ideas we hope to communicate in this book is that a *serious crisis is looming*, one that will adversely affect the life of every American. If U.S. businesses continue at the current rate to export jobs overseas, and more and more of our nation's adults allow themselves to be stuck in low-wage jobs or chronic unemployment, within two generations the United States will be a Third World country. Does that sound far-fetched? It is not. And the current trend will not reverse itself. Community by community, people must be willing to step forward and take decisive action.

If U.S. businesses continue at the current rate to export jobs overseas, and more and more of our nation's adults allow themselves to be stuck in low-wage jobs or chronic unemployment, within two generations the United States will be a Third World country. Does that sound far-fetched? It is not. And the current trend will not reverse itself.

The message of the ACP concept is this: The United States stands at a crossroad. We have two choices. We can allow current offshoring trends to continue or we can take immediate steps to produce the first-rate workforce that today's global economy demands. The first choice could eventually lead to economic ruin; the second gives us our best and only shot at sustainable prosperity. Proponents of ACP programs, representing all of the support "legs" we have discussed in this chapter, must be able to proclaim that message with clarity and passion.

BRINGING INFLUENTIAL PEOPLE TO THE TABLE

In this chapter we have suggested that, in the majority of cases, the best person to initiate an ACP effort will be the president of the local community or technical college. Regardless of who takes on that role, ACP proponents must be able to bring other leaders to the table. In the following two sections we provide steps for bringing those people together.

Convening Community Leaders

The following five steps form a general process for convening community leaders.

1. *Inventory the community, its industry, and its current workforce development and support structures*—In most cases, the local college will have access to the resources necessary to create a clear picture of all participants involved in building the ACP community.
2. *Determine which occupational clusters are needed*—This will vary community by community. The industry inventory (step 1) will provide a clear indication of which cluster should be targeted for the first ACP program.
3. *Identify the key persons within the four support "legs"*—This process should begin with employers but should also include other community leaders who have the authority and connections necessary to implement ACP.
4. *Establish a plan of action*—The plan will serve as the roadmap for implementation.
5. *Convene the top business leaders representing the identified cluster*—If the cluster has been well chosen—i.e., to reflect recognized workforce needs within the community—these leaders will come to the table with a shared sense of urgency.

Convening Business Representatives

Following is an adaptation of a six-stage process used by The Clements Group, L.C. of Salt Lake City. In this version it is assumed that the convener is a community college president and that the invitees are CEOs.

1. The college president and leadership team determine the top industry sectors currently driving the region's economy as well as those sectors that are projected to drive economic development of the region over the next five years.
2. The college's president invites an industry sector's CEOs to a two hour industry forum session to discuss industry challenges, economic development issues, labor pool climate, and workforce challenges, and to identify potential partnering areas.
3. Convene the industry CEOs with a facilitator to identify business, economic, and workforce concerns.
4. Prepare and disseminate a report of the outcome of the engagement, including the opportunity for participants to review the draft report prior to release to a wider audience of industry CEO's and community leaders, of the final draft of the Forum Report.
5. College president and leadership team review the report and determination of a proposed Industry Advancement Plan as a response to the Industry Forum Report including: identification of career ladder gaps and pathways, workforce skill and knowledge deficiency solutions, and development of potential college and industry partnering concepts and tactics to improve the industry's workforce.
6. An Industry Advancement Summit, a second engagement, is hosted by the college to convene the industry's CEOs to confirm the report findings, provide critical information about the college's current programs and services, review career ladder gaps and skills set solutions, confirm advancement concepts and tactics, and

define college and industry collaborative implementation roles, work groups, and timelines.

Early in the process of forming an ACP Partnership, the College CEO should name a member of the college staff to be the **ACP coordinator**. (Ultimately, this person may have a rank in the college similar to a dean.) In the formative stages, the ACP coordinator will be responsible for data gathering, meeting logistics, reports, publicity and other forms of communication. As the ACP program becomes a reality, the ACP coordinator will become the responsible manager of the organization and development/operation process, hiring staff, convening *second-level* meetings of faculty and employer representatives, building relationships with appropriate community leaders and searching for sources of state and federal funding.

Once assembled in common purpose, the partners must get to work. The new ACP partnership must get organized, set its goals and objectives and lay out a multiyear plan. The following chapters contain the elements and examples of a successful ACP program. We are not suggesting that it will be easy. We are suggesting that it must be done.

Chapter 5 Preview

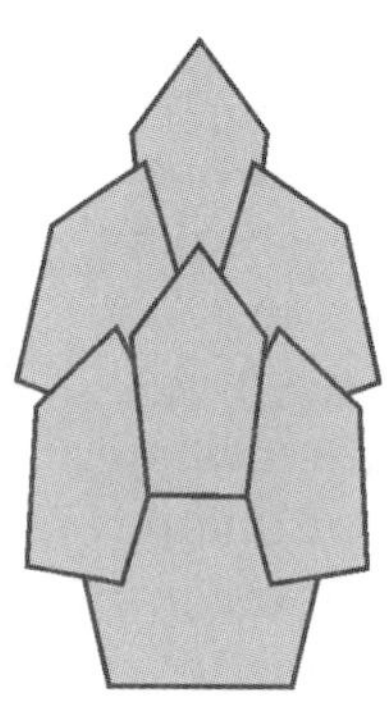

Successful ACP programs are "win-win" experiences for all interested parties, including communities, taxpayers, colleges, employers, and the ACP student-employees. But the most obvious winners are the student-employees and the participating employers; and these two groups will have to invest the greatest effort and/or resources to make ACP programs work. Chapters 6–8 outline the student commitment. This chapter attempts to describe in detail the efforts and resources that ACP employer partners will need to expend – and the benefits that they will reap. Every employer that considers participating in an ACP program will want to conduct a cost-versus-benefits analysis. Chapter 9, "Who Foots the Bill?," provides a list of employer costs and a framework to enable employers to determine cost per ACP student.

DH & RH

ORGANIZING EMPLOYERS FOR ADULT CAREER PATHWAYS

Dick Hinckley and Dan Hull

INTRODUCTION

Chapter 1 provides profiles of six broad groups of adults who need a second chance in public education. In many cases, perhaps most, the need is urgent. For all sorts of reasons—poor choices, poor schools, family circumstances, lack of guidance—millions of Americans function far below their abilities, and their numbers are growing daily. The cost to our society, both in lost productivity and in the tax burden of public assistance and containment, is enormous. Unless some kind of action is taken, right away, the downward trajectories of large and growing numbers of our citizens will only continue.

In the meantime, American employers also face a number of problems that are clearly getting worse:

- Rising costs
- Pressure to lower prices
- Increasing costs of healthcare

- Shortage of qualified hires
- A lack of experienced and skilled workers
- A labor pool with poor employability skills
- A labor pool in need of basic skills remediation
- Reduced worker productivity

That's a lot of bad news. And it's all the more discouraging when we consider that, in the preceding list of business woes, most of the items are "people problems." If we could poll America's business executives, they would probably say with one voice that they could deal with rising costs, foreign competition, government red tape, and any number of other pressures if they just didn't have so many problems with people. They can't find enough people, and the ones they *can* find are of poor quality.

If we could poll America's business executives, they would probably say with one voice that they could deal with rising costs, foreign competition, government red tape, and any number of other pressures if they just didn't have so many problems with people. They can't find enough people, and the ones they *can* find are of poor quality.

Alleviating "people problems" is what the ACP concept is all about. It is based on the presumption, borne out by the testimony of countless businesspeople, that large numbers of American citizens did not take full advantage of the benefits of a public education the first time they had the opportunity. Hence the widespread need for a "second chance." Fortunately, there's an encouraging way to spin the situation: As a group, the people who stand to benefit most from ACP programs represent a vast untapped resource that could become a powerful force in the U.S. economy. Many career-limited adults are capable learners and, with a little encouragement and tangible assistance, could become excellent employees in high-demand fields. The potential of America's citizenry is endless. The world has yet to see what the U.S. economy could accomplish if every American adult contributed to the extent of his or her ability.

As we have stated elsewhere in this book, most of the resources necessary to implement ACP programs are already in place. (See Appendix 5-2 for descriptions of two related programs.) Federal, state, community, and volunteer resources are available and could easily be redirected toward ACP. What is most urgently needed is a stronger commitment from the employer sector. Historically, employers have not taken a leading role in shaping the American workforce, and perhaps in times past there was no need for them to do so. But in today's global economy, employers must be willing to assume that role. Unless they do their fair share, we will not see significant changes in the quality of the American workforce any time soon, and employers will continue to struggle to find and keep the workers they need.

Please note that we are not asking that employers simply throw money at a problem. We are asking that they become *involved*. For that to happen, they must be willing to commit themselves from top to bottom, beginning at the highest levels in their leadership, the CEO. Participation in ACP programs will require changes in policies and procedures that only CEOs can authorize. But, even more important, CEOs set the tone for their organizations. If they can be won over to the ACP concept, it will become important to the people under their authority. We stress this point here, at the outset of this chapter, to ensure that one point is absolutely clear: Participation in ACP programs will require more than sending one or two middle managers to periodic meetings. It will require fundamental changes that can only come from the top.

We are not asking that employers simply throw money at a problem. We are asking that they become *involved*. For that to happen, they must be willing to commit themselves from top to bottom, beginning at the highest levels in their leadership, the CEO.

This chapter has three purposes: (1) to describe an adaptable, generic ACP model, giving special emphasis to the role of employers; (2) to describe what we call the "nuts and bolts" of employer involvement; and (3) to describe some of the key benefits that ACP programs offer to their employer partners.

Our audience is twofold: First, we are also speaking directly to employers: The information provided in this chapter will show what it would take for an employer to become a full-fledged partner in an ACP program, and what that employer could expect to gain in return. Second, we hope to provide ACP coordinators with information that will help them as they promote the ACP concept among potential employer partners. As we attempt to clarify in this chapter, ACP coordinators must be sensitive to the concerns of the potential employer partners they hope to enlist. This point was recently emphasized in a communication to us from Rick Stephens, Senior Vice President for Human Resources at the Boeing Company. According to Stephens, potential employer partners will rightfully insist that four elements be in place before they will commit to the program:

- A shared willingness to develop a *common language and vocabulary* that will enable business, education, and community partners to communicate with one another
- A clear understanding of the *motivation* of each of the partners (Why are they involved? What do they hope to gain?)
- Agreement on expected *outcomes,* to ensure alignment and integration of stakeholders' end product needs
- Clear evidence that the proposed program will *increase worker productivity*

A GENERIC MODEL FOR EMPLOYER INVOLVEMENT

No two ACP programs will be exactly alike. The development and administrative processes involved will vary according to local factors. Nevertheless, all ACP programs will follow certain general steps and exhibit the same basic characteristics. The following ten points provide an adaptable, generic ACP model from the employer partner's perspective. (Points 7 and 8 refer to specific numbers of hours of part-time study. The numbers chosen are such that, by the end of Stage 10, an ACP student-employee would have completed enough hours to earn an associate degree.)

1. *ACP programs are developed by colleges, but their focus and content are strongly influenced by local employers.* As noted in Chapter 4, the logical persons to lead in the development of ACP programs are community and technical college presidents. We ended that chapter with a description of a process that college presidents can use to convene business leaders for the purpose of identifying their workforce needs. The ACP concept asks that colleges make significant changes in the way they approach businesses. Rather than promoting their own programs and services as "business solutions," as is typically done, the ACP concept asks that colleges convene businesses specifically for the purpose of voicing their (the businesses') needs and concerns. In turn, the participating businesses should come to table with the understanding that their input will drive the resulting career ladders and community response. They should also understand that their input will be expected on a continuing basis.
2. *Every ACP program focuses on a single employment sector such as healthcare, telecommunication, financial services, IT, or hospitality.* The power of the ACP approach derives in part from the fact that it brings together people with sharply focused expertise in the employment clusters they represent. At the same time, those people are sensitive to the characteristics of their communities and how their organizations serve (and are served by) those communities. This level of expertise enables ACP advisory boards, curriculum committees, and other groups to ensure that the ACP programs they develop and oversee meet the needs of all parties involved—not only ACP student-employees but also their employers, their colleges, and other entities that support them along the way. The involvement of *local* employers is necessary to determine which sectors will be addressed in any given setting. While workers in some occupational fields

are needed virtually everywhere—healthcare and information technology, for example—many communities have one or more industry sectors that require relatively large numbers of specialized workers. Those sectors will determine the content and focus of the ACP programs that serve them.

3. *Participating employers identify the skills that workers in their sectors should posses.* In the previous item, we noted that the participation of local employers is necessary to ensure that the ACP program(s) developed corresponds to areas in which workers are in short supply, locally. The next step in that process is to identify the skills (and certificates) that are required in the sectors being addressed. For example, if nurse supervision is identified as an area of need, representatives of that sector would jointly compile a list of the qualities, both technical and interpersonal, that nurse supervisors should possess. Identification of those qualities helps to ensure that ACP curricula prepare student-employees for the tasks that lie ahead of them, and that the student-employees possess the skills their employers expect.
4. *Participating employers jointly create career ladders that identify what ACP student-employees must do to move upward incrementally in the workplace. Career ladders identify the skills that must be demonstrated before moving from each level to the next, and how progress is acknowledged and rewarded by the employer (which includes certifications, in some cases).* Almost every business has some kind of career ladder, that is, a series of employment "rungs" that employees climb as they gain in expertise and the value they bring to their employers. The ACP concept asks that, for any given program, employers in the same sector *jointly* develop a shared career ladder to which they are all willing to adhere. One of the key elements of the ACP concept is that it calls for numerous intermediate goals as the student-employee works his or her way through the ACP stages. By acknowledging advancement from one rung to the next, participating

employers motivate their ACP student-employees to persevere and complete their programs. To avoid confusion and frustration among student-employees, the employer partners for any given ACP programs should agree to use the *same* career ladder, to ensure that student-employees are rewarded in the same ways and for the same accomplishments.

In the preceding remarks we have repeatedly stressed the importance of focusing on *local* employment needs. While that is an essential aspect of the ACP concept, ACP programs should also be designed to help their students meet standards that are recognized within their industries as a whole. (Ideally, every ACP program would lead to an AAS degree.) The ladder curricula followed in ACP program courses should reflect both local needs and standards established by national accrediting boards and industry regulatory groups. Similarly, every career ladder should specify continuing education requirements for licenses and certifications and what constitutes professional growth in the sector to which it applies. (For more on career ladders and ladder curricula, see Chapter 8.)

5. *Colleges assume the responsibility of recruiting ACP students and preparing them for entry-level employment. (This constitutes a screening process that greatly benefits the employer partners.)* All across the nation, employers complain that job applicants do not know how to interview, lack even the most basic communication skills, and do not understand the demands of daily work. ACP programs can help to reduce the time and effort employers spend on unsuitable job applicants by screening prospective employees *before* they arrive at the workplace. Employers should see this as a considerable benefit. ACP student-employees who come to their premises to work will have already eliminated most academic deficiencies and received training in employability skills.

We make no attempt here to assign a dollar value to this benefit, but employers should be able to do so, treating it as a percentage of their human resources budgets. (To see how projected savings in human resources activities would compare to the overall cost to employers of participation in ACP programs, see Chapter 9. For more on recruitment and assessment of ACP candidates, see Chapter 6.)

In reciprocation, employers should be expected to assist in the recruiting process by providing names of applicants who were not hired. In most cases, those people would be ACP candidates. Extending this process one step further, the employers could share aggregate information about the applicants that would help ACP coordinators know what steps should be taken to make those people more employable.

6. *Participating employers interview and hire ACP students after they have completed Stage 1 (one semester of full-time coursework at the partnering college). New hires begin at the bottom of the career ladder. For any given ACP program, all employer partners agree to use the* <u>*same*</u> *ladder.* By agreeing to support ACP, employer partners are committing to hire ACP student-employees after one semester of college coursework. That's a big commitment, but it should involve very little risk to the employers. Students who prove themselves work-ready by completing ACP Stage 1 will have been screened, will have eliminated their academic deficiencies, and will have had practice in demonstrating good work habits. Through guidance counseling and career exploration activities, they will have become familiar with long-term career opportunities that interest them, and will have acquired a sense of what it takes to achieve long-term career goals.

   When the students have completed Stage 1, they are interviewed by the employer partners for part-jobs in their chosen pathways. (Stage 2 combines part-time work and part-time schooling.) This juncture represents one of several points in the ACP process at which employers must resist the temptation to compete. They must agree to a common set of guidelines for interviewing and hiring so that the ACP student-employees in their employment sectors are treated consistently from worksite to worksite—and they must agree not to try to lure student-employees away from one another. The college, acting as the neutral party, can assist in the interviewing and hiring process.

7. *During Stage 2, ACP student-employees work part-time for the employer partners (30 hours per week) while taking 9 credit hours at the college. The employers pay for tuition and allow each student-employee one hour per day of paid release time to attend classes.* Stage 2 of the ACP process represents a rigorous program of study and work that can test the student-employees' resolve and endurance. Employers must have the patience to let the plan work, offering encouragement and guidance. During this stage, mentors (selected from among the employer partners' full-time workers) should establish positive relationships with the student-employees to ensure that they settle into routines that are conducive to success. Stage 2 is a make-or-break stage. Student-employees who make it through Stage 2 have a high likelihood of completing their programs.
8. *During Stages 3–10, ACP student-employees work full-time while taking 6 credit hours per term at the college. Employers provide employee benefits, tuition, and 2 hours per day of paid release time to attend classes.* Like Stage 2, as described in the previous point, Stages 3–10 will call for patience and encouragement on the part of employers. The suggested release time also represents a real cost to the employers, but it is a smart investment that will pay dividends over time. Student-employees who make it to Stage 3 and beyond will have demonstrated tenacity, loyalty, and commitment. Employers must be able to resist the temptation to push them too hard in the near term. Patience is the key.

9. *Each time an ACP student-employee progresses from one ACP stage to the next – i.e., moves up a rung on the career ladder – he or she should be recognized and rewarded by the participating employer.* One of the most important ways employers contribute to the success of ACP programs is to provide incentives for student-employees to keep pressing on to the next levels. The reward can take any of several forms, from salary raises to changes in title or responsibilities. Even a simple gesture such as an announcement in a company newsletter or certificate of achievement can make a big difference in the attitudes of student-employees. In any case, the career ladder should be replete with points at which the employee is recognized for continued participation and achievement. The proverbial light at the end of the tunnel will be dim in the early stages, so whatever the employer can do to encourage the employee and recognize achievement levels will be critical to success. This is an area in which competitors must be willing to cooperate. If one employer gives ACP student-employees a raise when they move from, say, Stage 3 to Stage 4 but another merely acknowledges the accomplishment in some intangible way, resentment may result. The system of awards should be uniform throughout each ACP program.
10. *Participating employers must agree not to attempt to hire ACP student-employees away from one another.* The need to find good employees may sometimes be so great that employers are tempted to entice ACP student-employees away from competitors with higher pay or other benefits. In some cases, student-employees would be easy prey, especially if the incentive is higher pay. Left unchecked, this practice will completely undermine any ACP program. If employers see that the time, effort, and money they invest ultimately serve other businesses rather than their own, they will drop out of the program. Great restraint will be required on both sides. Students should be counseled to stay focused on their futures and

not to accept short-term gain at the expense of long-term fulfillment.

Another temptation to which students may be subject is this: It's not uncommon for community college students to leave technical degree programs after completing three or four courses. In some situations, that amount of coursework is enough to become employable at respectable wages. But over time, the skills that made those students employable become outmoded and they are laid off. The employer must seek new workers, and the former employee, now unemployed, is prevented from going back school because of the family commitments that he or she has since taken on. No one wins. The ACP concept calls upon all participants to take the long view, deferring short-term rewards for the sake of long-term (even lifelong) fulfillment. Keeping an eye on the ultimate outcome is critical.

Potential employer partners will rightfully insist that four elements be in place before they will commit to the program:

- A shared willingness to develop a *common language and vocabulary* that will enable business, education, and community partners to communicate with one another
- A clear understanding of the *motivation* of each of the partners (Why are they involved? What do they hope to gain?)
- Agreement on expected *outcomes,* to ensure alignment and integration of stakeholders' end product needs
- Clear evidence that the proposed program will *increase worker productivity*

Rick Stephens
Senior Vice President for Human Resources
The Boeing Company

THE NUTS AND BOLTS OF EMPLOYER COMMITMENT

Part of what we are asking employers to commit is philosophical. We are asking them to buy into an *idea,* and then to do whatever they can to help others in their organizations and their employment sectors to buy into that idea as well. This is why the complete commitment of CEOs is so critical. To a large extent, they shape the philosophies of their companies.

Yet most of the specific, detailed work—the nuts and bolts of developing and maintaining ACP programs—will be carried out by lower-ranking employees. Some of the work is mundane, from attending meetings to reviewing policies and making phone calls. But it is no less important. It requires talent and dedication. Part of what we are asking employers to do is to commit some of the time of their best employees to the carrying out of the normal, everyday tasks associated with developing and running ACP programs.

The specifics will vary from place to place and program to program, but the employer partners for every ACP program should plan to commit personnel who can cover at least the following four areas:

1. *Participation in the creation of the program, including the program's career ladder and ladder curriculum.* Within practically every company there are employees who understand and can *describe* the skills that the company requires throughout its ranks. They are the people who should be chosen to participate in creation of the program's career ladder and ladder curriculum. In most cases, frontline supervisors are *not* good choices to fill this role, since few will have the required knowledge of their employers' operations overall. Mid-level managers and higher are usually better choices. Whoever is chosen, it should be someone who understands the importance of long-term employee goals and progression and is comfortable working with community college faculty members. Both in teaching and ladder curriculum development, the program's faculty members must know exactly what the employer partners expect their workers to know and be able to do. Part of the "nuts and bolts" of

participation is to communicate that information clearly, as it pertains to both soft skills and technical skills.

Every employer partner should also expect to devote a certain amount of employee time to the development of the program's career ladder. For every ACP program, someone must decide on a system of rewards and incentives to be granted as student-employees move up the career ladder. As the process unfolds, employers may find that the services required involve a whole range of departments, from human resources to accounting to frontline production workers. In any case, the task should be approached with energy and a sense of creativity.

2. *Selection and hiring of ACP students after completion of Stage 1.* Stage 1 constitutes a screening process. Completers of Stage 1 have eliminated their academic deficiencies, they have been counseled, and they have undergone employability training. They are ready for work in their chosen fields.

   The assignment of ACP student-employees to employers should be made through a mutually recognized arrangement involving the college and all of the employer partners. Some of the employers may have strict drug policies while others have strict policies on the handling of personal information or insurance issues. Because of those differences, a master agreement should be drawn up and signed by the parties involved. Having a written agreement that has been negotiated by all the employer partners will also help to guard against competition for student-employees.

3. *Supporting, mentoring, and rewarding ACP student-employees throughout the three-year span of their programs.* As stated earlier, ACP student-employees and the employer partners alike must exercise restraint: They must resist the temptation to terminate programs prematurely for the sake of short-term gain. ACP programs have the potential to repay employer outlays many times over, but only if they are considered as long-

term investments. If the ACP concept catches on to the extent that we envision, the time will come when it will be possible to perform cost-benefit analyses based on hard data. We are confident that the results of those analyses will bear out our contention that employer investment in ACP programs represents a smart business strategy.

As described in item 1 on the previous page, employer partners should expect to reward their ACP student-employees often, at least every time they move up on the career ladder. This represents a cost to the employer in two ways: First, someone has to spend time devising a system of rewards, *in conjunction with other employers in the program.* (Remember: The career ladder must be uniform throughout the program.) Second, while it is not necessary that all rewards have cash value—write-ups in company newsletters, for example—some of them definitely should. Somewhere along the way every ACP student-employee who continues stage after stage to meet his or her obligations should receive a bonus, a raise, a promotion, or some other tangible reward. Employers should also be conscientious in acknowledging student-employees' progress in meeting the requirements for standardized certifications and credentials.

Every ACP student-employee will require an employee mentor after Stage 1, especially during the earlier stages. This represents a real cost to the employer, who must be willing to provide the necessary paid release time.

4. *Willingness to negotiate and enter formal "will-not-compete" agreements stating that employer partners will not compete for student-employees.* One of the characteristics of the generic ACP program model we presented in a previous section is that the employer partners agree not to compete with one another for student-employees. We bring the issue up again here because it has a "nuts and bolts" aspect. "Will-not-compete" agreements don't just happen, especially in situations in which worker shortages are

acute, as is often the case in certain categories of healthcare workers. The agreements must be negotiated, drawn up, reviewed, revised, and so on, and that effort takes time that represents a real cost to the employer partners. The partners must be willing to accept that cost. All of the partners have a vested interest in the success of their programs as a whole. All will benefit from an increase in the availability of well-qualified workers. The situation is a perfect illustration of the old adage that a rising tide lifts all boats.

HOW WILL PARTICIPATING EMPLOYERS BENEFIT FROM ACP PROGRAMS?

ACP programs offer many benefits to their employer partners. In fact, we consider this one of the strongest selling points of the ACP concept—that by helping others through their support for ACP programs, employer partners bring lasting benefits to themselves.

Specifically, ACP programs, implemented on a large scale, could reverse some of the most troubling trends in the American workplace. Consider the list of business problems presented on the first two pages of this chapter:

- *Employers say they can't find enough good workers.* One of main objectives of the ACP concept is to enlarge the pool of high-quality workers who are available locally. The ACP concept calls for a strong recruiting component that reaches out to people who are capable of doing ACP-level postsecondary coursework but who are reluctant to pursue college without help and encouragement. We believe that *many* career-limited adults fall into that category.
- *Employers complain that the only people they can hire are of poor quality.* ACP will focus specifically on preparing students to be conscientious, productive workers. Those who see their programs through to completion will be first-rate employees in their sectors.

- *Employers complain that their new hires can't read, communicate, or do simple math.* A major portion of ACP Stage 1 is devoted to dealing with these deficiencies. In fact, some remediation will take place before prospective ACP students even enter Stage 1. By the time they enter the workplace, at the beginning of Stage 2, they should possess good core academic skills that they continue to build on over time.
- *Employers need greater productivity from their workers to allow them to compete in a world economy.* ACP will reduce the cost of recruitment, training, and employee turnover. It will provide pre-screened employees ready and able to meet the demands of the workplace. Ultimately, it will moderate pressures on unrealistic salaries as the labor pool is increased.

It is not our purpose to present the ACP concept as a panacea. Nevertheless, we believe that ACP programs have the potential to alleviate virtually all of the persistent "people problems" that plague American employers. It won't happen overnight. But it shouldn't take a generation either. In the case of well-established programs, employer partners should expect to see a return on their investment within the first two years. This is because ACP student-employees who have stuck it out to the Stages 6, 7, and 8 should already be strong, productive employees. Those who demonstrate the strength of character necessary to complete their programs should be first-rate technicians that any employer would be proud to claim.

APPENDIX 5-1: A CHECKLIST OF ACTION ITEMS FOR EMPLOYER PARTNERS

1. Develop and agree upon the career ladder(s) needed by industry. For each career cluster area, the career ladder must be devised and agreed upon.
    a. Form a career ladder task group with college and business membership
    b. Work through the Ladder Curriculum Design as provided in Chapter 8

   c. Agree upon the curriculum and commission the assembly of the courses, certificates, and degrees
   d. Establish the delivery mechanisms
   e. Train the instructional staff as needed

2. Inventory the community for existing public and private programs for services required to assist students through the stages. For each stage and potential student support need, form a matrix matching existing programs and services to the need areas
   a. Form a support program task group with college, business, and community membership
   b. Identify gaps in services
   c. Prepare a plan to address the gaps

3. Develop a capital campaign. With the college president and other community leaders, develop the capital campaign to raise local dollars to support the needs of the students as identified in the gap analysis above
   a. Work with consultants on a capital campaign plan
   b. Establish support structures to administer services to students

4. Provide opportunities for students and new employees. For each job position, establish the business support structures.
   a. Determine where and when internships will be provided
   b. Establish a mentor program

APPENDIX 5-2: EXAMPLES OF INDUSTRY GROUPS WHOSE GOALS PARALLEL THOSE OF ACP

One of the main premises underlying the ACP concept is that it is consistent with many workforce development activities that are already taking place. Our intent in presenting the concept in this book is not to compete with other initiatives but to provide a blueprint for combining resources and achieving a new level of collaboration, especially between the public and private sectors. Following are short descriptions of two organizations whose activities are consistent with the ACP concept.

MEP: The Manufacturing Extension Partnership

MEP is a nationwide network of nearly 350 not-for-profit centers whose sole purpose is to help small and medium-sized manufacturers. The centers, serving all 50 States and Puerto Rico, are linked through the Department of Commerce's National Institute of Standards and Technology. Like ACP programs, MEP centers are funded by a combination of federal, state, local, and private resources. Each center works directly with area manufacturers to provide expertise and services tailored to their most critical needs. Solutions are offered through a combination of direct assistance from center staff and outside consultants.

> **Without well-trained employees who are capable of learning and growing with their organizations, U.S. manufacturers cannot survive.**
>
> **Roy Peters**
> **President, Oklahoma Manufacturing Alliance**

One of MEP's main focuses is worker training, an area of urgent need in every part of the country. Roy Peters, President of the Oklahoma Manufacturing Alliance, an MEP Center, stated in a recent interview that "the biggest problem facing U.S. manufacturers is the availability of qualified employees. Manufacturers are turning down work or outsourcing production because the available workforce lacks quantity and quality."

Peters went on to sound this ominous note: "Without well-trained employees who are capable of learning and growing with their organizations, U.S. manufacturers cannot survive."

Like ACP and many other initiatives around the country, MEP represents a promising avenue of opportunity for collaboration between educators, employers, government agencies, and community and faith-based organizations. "We must find a way to stop the loss of American jobs to overseas workers," Peters insisted. "It will be expensive, but it will cost us a lot less than paying taxes to support the unemployed, underemployed, and incarcerated."

The Texas Business and Education Coalition (TBEC)

TBEC was formed in 1989 to help Texas public schools meet the employment needs of the state's increasingly diverse economy. As a result of TBEC's efforts, student achievement has improved, along with the state's workforce. Nevertheless, thousands of good jobs remain unfilled because too many adults lack the knowledge, skills, work habits, and personal qualities required in today's workplace.

Governor Rick Perry's Industry Cluster Initiative has further increased the demand for scientists, engineers, technicians, and other highly skilled workers in advanced technologies such as aerospace, biotechnology, defense, energy, and information technology.[1] To address this situation, in 2006 TBEC leaders refocused the coalition's mission on connecting education more directly to the state's emerging job market and economic development goals. Part of that process, they recognized, would involve working to remove the negative stigma that is often attached to career and technical education (CTE). TBEC believes that this perception can be changed only by implementing academically rigorous grade-9–14 Career Pathways, as described in the predecessor to this book, *Career Pathways: Education with a Purpose* (CORD, 2005).

TBEC also recognizes that Texas cannot afford to wait until today's middle and high school students have made their way through a reformed public education system. The current and short-term needs of the state's employers can be met only by improving the skills and work-readiness of adults who were not well served by public education, or succeeded in public education but are still not prepared to compete in the global economy. In TBEC's view, the solution is Adult Career Pathways. (Source: John Stevens, Executive Director, TBEC)

---

[1] For more on the initiative, visit http://www.governor.state.tx.us/divisions/press/initiatives/Industry_Cluster/Industry_Cluster_SP/.

Chapter 6 Preview

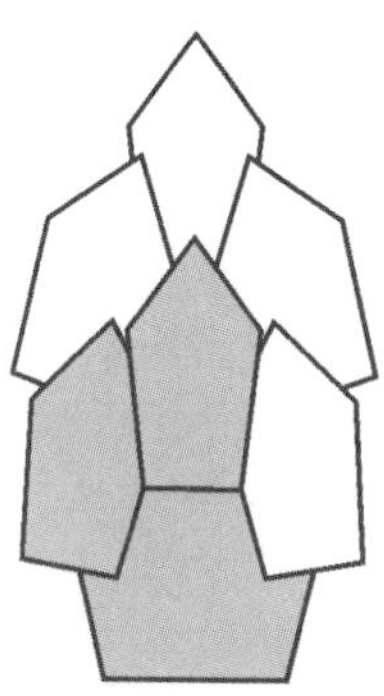

Community colleges are either not receiving or not retaining most adults who are candidates for ACP programs. Many adults are not aware of the opportunities for career preparation available at the colleges or do not feel that they are "college material." Unique, proactive recruiting efforts will be required to reach these people. Many of the ones who do apply are discouraged by the testing process, or upon finding out that they are not ready or when they realize the time and cost required; consequently, either they do not register or they drop out early in their first courses. Recruiting and assessing students for ACP programs is a major effort.

Not all ACP applicants will be ready for the Prep Phase and, for various reasons, some may never be acceptable candidates.

This chapter attempts to identify where ACP candidates can be located and recruited. It also outlines qualifications for acceptance into an ACP program.

DH & RH

Recruiting and Assessing Students

Anthony Iacono and Dan Hull

By definition, all Adult Career Pathways students will be *nontraditional students.* Broadly speaking, the term *nontraditional student* applies to any student who doesn't "fit the model" for traditional students. In our culture it is generally expected that students graduate from high school and proceed directly to college, completing associate degrees in two years and/or bachelor's degrees in four or five years. A student who follows that model is considered *traditional.* More specifically, the traditional student—

1. Decides upon a field of study before entering college or while enrolled in college and completes a degree in that field before entering the workforce full-time. (Traditional students are more or less the same age as the students with whom they attend classes and graduate.)
2. Is prepared academically (by the end of high school) to enter and succeed in a postsecondary course of study.
3. Has or is able to obtain the financial resources necessary to attend college.

4. Is at least reasonably proficient in core academic subjects and is capable of learning in conventional educational environments based on textbooks and lectures.

In comparing the preceding four traits with the characteristics of our target population, as described in Chapter 1, the reader will readily see that the career-limited adults who most stand to benefit from ACP are *all* nontraditional in some way. They have not graduated from high school, or they have not acquired enough college credits to be of any long-term value, or they have language or academic difficulties that impede their educational progress, or they have gotten into legal difficulties—and so on. In those cases, the normal flow—from high school to college to work—has been interrupted.

As Chapter 1 also points out, the number of career-limited adults in the United States is large—running into the millions—and growing. But how do we find those people and get them into ACP programs? That's the first challenge, and it's a difficult one.

In this chapter we examine two broad recruiting fields—on-campus and off-campus. We focus on community and technical college campuses because many ACP candidates are already there, or at least they have had formal contact with the colleges and are in the colleges' databases. Every community and technical college has records of people who have applied but never enrolled, taken (but failed) proficiency exams, taken courses but not completed degrees, and/or dropped out of classes. **Those are ACP candidates.** The barriers to their academic and career progress may be daunting—financial, academic, personal, legal—but the authors are of the firm conviction that, by and large, those people represent a vast untapped resource. With help, many, if not most, are capable of acquiring postsecondary knowledge and skills that will prepare them for rewarding careers. But they cannot be helped via ACP programs until they have been identified, recruited into the programs, and given the assistance necessary to overcome the barriers that have thus far held them back. Consequently, recruiting is a matter of great urgency and should be a primary focus of every ACP program.

Along with recruiting, ACP programs must be equipped to assess potential candidates. Although many career-limited adults have the native ability and determination to thrive in ACP programs, some do not. Sorting those people out early in the process is important—for the good of both the unsuccessful candidate and the ACP program.

The authors envision a four-step recruiting and assessment process. The four steps, as outlined in Figure 6-1, are the following:

- Locate ACP candidates
- Recruit ACP candidates
- Assess and select ACP students
- Prepare selected students to enter ACP programs

RECRUITING: WHERE DO WE FIND ACP CANDIDATES?

Unlike the grade-9–14 Career Pathways model, whose purpose is to help high school students transition to and succeed in career-focused college programs immediately following high school graduation, ACP has the more difficult goal of helping adults who have taken life-changing detours and need a second chance to reenter and reach their potential in education and careers.[1] The first challenge of ACP is identifying candidates. Some have already established relationships with colleges; others have not.

In discussing recruiting in the following sections, we focus on two broad populations: (1) people who have already established contact with community and technical colleges (through enrollment, application, or some other formal means) and (2) people of whom the colleges have no record.

---

[1] For more on grade-9–14 Career Pathways, see Dan Hull et al., *Career Pathways: Education with a Purpose* (CORD, 2005).

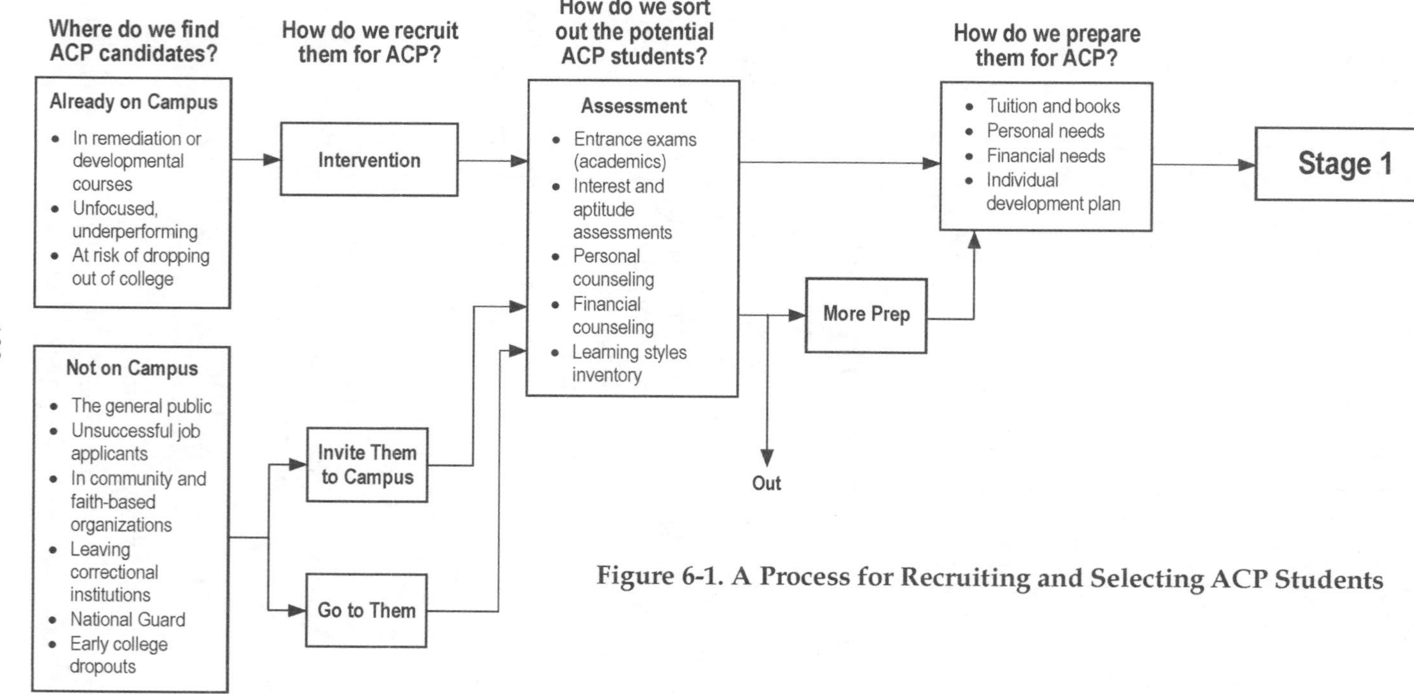

Figure 6-1. A Process for Recruiting and Selecting ACP Students

Recruiting from College Students and Applicants

Virtually every community college in the country is attended, or has been applied to, or has administered placement exams to, potential ACP candidates. Those candidates comprise three subgroups: (1) applicants whose low placement test scores call for remediation, (2) applicants who have no idea what fields of study they are interested in pursuing, and (3) students in their first or second terms who are performing poorly and are at risk of dropping out.

Let's look at how those three subgroups might be approached by ACP programs.

1. *Applicants who score poorly on the college's placement tests and are advised that they must take one or more remedial courses in English, mathematics, and/or science*

   The obvious strategy in this situation is to make judgments about students' potential strictly on the basis of test scores, and that's exactly what happens in most community college settings. But the ACP concept calls for looking a little deeper and maybe even a little "hand holding." Every college in America has a guidance department whose role is to guide students through their degree programs. In most cases, guidance departments are passive, in the sense that they wait for students to come to them. That works fine for most traditional students, but ACP candidates often need what we might call *proactive guidance*. Failing a college proficiency exam is discouraging to any student, but for many potential ACP candidates it may the "last straw" that causes them to conclude, once and for all, that they are not college material. In most colleges, there is virtually no connection between assessment centers and guidance offices. College guidance counselors are there for people who *enroll*, not for people who fail proficiency exams and walk away. Consequently, many people who would benefit from the second chance that ACP programs offer—and might be steered in that direction by guidance counselors—never even see counselors. Compounding the problem, more and more colleges allow students to skip one-on-one counseling sessions by allowing them to declare majors and register online.

Nontraditional students require nontraditional counseling. Even strong traditional students can be intimidated by the "take a number and have a seat" approach to counseling. To ensure that nontraditional students (ACP candidates) are aware of *all* the opportunities available to them, guidance counselors must go to the students, not wait for the students to come to them. A student who thinks he or she may have just failed a placement test should not be expected to proceed immediately to a guidance office across campus, without knowing the result of the test or the implications of success or failure. Counselors should meet students in the assessment centers immediately upon test completion. This would provide an opportunity for the counselor to shake the student's hand and say, "Even if you failed this test, you have options. Let's explore them. Don't be discouraged."

2. *Applicants who have no idea what field of study they are interested in pursuing*

   Many young people apply to college by default: They think it's expected, and nothing else appeals to them. Experience has shown that, for the most part, those students are unfocused and, therefore, uninterested in college. Allowing them to register for general classes usually just postpones the inevitable. Because they have no real interest in their studies, they eventually stop attending classes and flunk out. ACP programs would engage those students in assessments, experiences, and activities that would give them a sense of purpose in higher education by helping them to identify their aptitudes and interests.

3. *Students in their first or second terms who are performing poorly and are at risk of dropping out*

   Identifying and capturing these students before they walk away forever close coordination between faculty members and counselors. Guidance offices should not be physically remote from faculty offices. They should be right alongside each other. Such an arrangement would allow faculty members and counselors to work closely together. (In today's academic world, the two groups rarely even know each other, much less work together.) When an instructor becomes aware that a student is unable to learn course material, has substandard attendance, or exhibits any other behavior that is likely to lead to failure in that course, the instructor could immediately take the student to a counselor. A good counselor, working closely with the instructor, could help the student find purpose in education by recruiting him or her into an ACP program.

Recruiting from Adults in the Community Who Are Not Associated with the College

While many potential ACP candidates will have left some kind of trail at community colleges, others will never have set foot on a college campus. Following are suggestions for ways to identify and attract those people:

1. *Advertise in the community*—Every ACP program should have a marketing plan that makes effective use of standard advertising media such as newspapers, radio, television, and the Internet. The advertisements should stress benefits that are attractive to career-limited adults—higher pay, interesting work, hands-on learning environments that do not require extensive reading, opportunities for advancement with benefits, and, perhaps most important, help with personal expenses during the first semester of school. Better still, participating employers could state in their "help wanted" advertisements that vacancies will be filled by students in certain ACP programs. Civic and faith-based organizations can also play a role. Every community has numerous civic and faith-based organizations that would be willing to provide bulletin board and newsletter space for information about ACP programs. (Many would also

be willing to provide meeting rooms so that potential ACP candidates could meet counselors on their own turf, so to speak. See also number 2, below, and Chapter 12.) In any case, every advertisement should call attention to the availability of counseling and willingness of program personnel to meet with the potential candidate face to face.

2. *Meet with leaders of civic and faith-based organizations to explain the ACP program and enlist their advocacy, partnership, and support*—Civic and faith-based organizations represent a huge recruiting opportunity for ACP programs. In most cases, they will readily commit to partnering with ACP programs because, ultimately, their goal is the same as that of ACP—to better the lives of people who need a little extra help in reaching their potential. This is discussed and expanded upon in Chapter 12.
3. *Contact urban housing authorities* - Housing subsidies often come with the stipulation that the recipient must also enroll in classes on financial management and take additional classes designed to provide basic educational or workforce skills. The opportunity to gain technical skills and earn significantly above minimum wage should appeal to most residents of subsidized housing communities, especially given the added benefit of financial assistance. Because ACP programs and housing authorities have compatible goals, partnerships should be easy to create.
4. *Contact people who applied for jobs with the participating employers but were not selected* - Historically, colleges have not always found employers to be cooperative in sharing this information. But ACP employer partners will have a clear understanding of the benefits to themselves of cooperating in this manner. This is also discussed in Chapter 5.
5. *Corrections agencies*—Corrections and law enforcement agencies provide a valuable, though sometimes difficult, recruiting opportunity. Unfortunately, successful reentry

of ex-offenders is often impeded by fear of recidivism: Many people balk at the mere suggestion of programs that mix ex-offenders with the general public. Nevertheless, successful reentry programs and strategies exist and should be leveraged to enable ex-offenders to have the second chance in education to which every American citizen is entitled. It is to the advantage of every member of society to help these individuals reenter society in a manner that is positive and productive.

Recruitment efforts should focus on state and federal prisons, rather than city and county jails, which are typically used only for temporary incarceration. The best candidates for ACP programs would be inmates who have taken advantage of education programs while in prison and are within six months of parole. Correctional education programs are generally geared toward adult basic education and GED attainment, which are at about the same level as the first stage of the career ladder. Some inmates will also have been involved in college credit career programs that qualify them for more advanced placement on the career ladder.

The following should be considered when recruiting from corrections facilities:

- Contact local offices of the state's corrections parole services to offer ACP options to their placement services.
- Prepare a list of companies that are within the targeted ACP clusters for jobs they are willing and able to offer to parolees.
- Work through issues of company liability, supervision, and legal/appropriate disclosures of worker backgrounds.
- Work with the parole services on issues relating to notification of local police authorities as to the placement of parolees.

- Contact local chapters of prisoner advocacy groups for supporting partnership opportunities, programs, and services.

Ex-offenders should be carefully screened before being admitted to ACP programs. The screening process should meet the following criteria:

- Persons with convictions for sex crimes, violent offenses, or felony drug crimes should not be considered. Most employers will refuse to hire them. (Maintaining strong relationships with employer partners is essential. Dissatisfaction on their part could lead to the demise of the program as a whole.)
- Every participating inmate must be made aware that, once released, he or she must work closely with a support team that includes a probation officer.
- Every participating inmate must be made aware that violation of probation or additional arrests will terminate his or her participation in the program.

Although some industries, such as healthcare, may not be willing to grant internships to candidates with problematic backgrounds, other industries may be more lenient. The key to helping parolees succeed in the program is to allow employers to have the ultimate say in who is allowed onto their premises. Any attempt to force a person on a company will create an atmosphere of ill will and distrust. In those situations, no one benefits.

6. *National Guard Centers*—Unlike full-time soldiers, guardsmen do not routinely spend extended periods of time overseas or in remote environments in which technology is not readily available. Except in extraordinary circumstances, their commitment involves on a few weeks a year. Since military recruiters often struggle to meet their monthly quotas, and the armed forces routinely offer educational incentives in their recruiting campaigns, it is likely that the National Guard will want to participate in ACP programs. Partnership with the guard could work on two levels:

a. ACP classes, especially Internet classes, could be offered as incentives for enlistment.

b. The National Guard should look favorably upon (and be willing to promote) any apprenticeship-style program that enhances the technical skills of its members.

The Key to Recruiting Good Candidates Is to Recruit Committed *Partners*

The avenues for recruitment of ACP candidates are limited only by the imagination of the ACP staff. Nevertheless, success in recruiting will depend ultimately on the level of commitment of each program's partners. The key to success is persuading others—especially employers and community leaders—to buy into the ACP concept. The way to do this is to help potential partners see that ACP programs offer significant benefits to every entity involved. If employers can be made to see that supporting ACP programs is a smart *business* decision, they will support them. If faith-based organizations can be made to see that supporting ACP programs helps them accomplish *their* mission, they too will support them, as will colleges and government agencies and any number of other potential partners. With ample support, the ACP concept has the potential to offer career-limited Americans better lives—and a way to give something back to the entities that helped them.

ASSESSMENT: HOW DO WE RECOGNIZE ACP CANDIDATES?

Following are guidelines for identifying suitable ACP candidates and counseling them during the enrollment process:

1. Obtain general information about the candidate. For example, if the candidate has applied to or enrolled in a college, the college should have records of items such as placement test scores and major(s) declared.

2. In interviewing the candidate, present an overview of the ACP concept. The candidate should be made to understand that the focus of the first semester is coursework (rather than employment) and that living expenses will be provided. The counselor should also explain that, after the first semester, the candidate/student will begin working in a selected field such as engineering, healthcare, or information technology. Upon completion of the program (7–10 stages), the candidate/student will be hired full-time by the company where he or she worked part-time during the program.
3. Determine the candidate's financial need. This can be done by having the candidate complete a FAFSA (Free Application for Federal Student Aid) and an application to the college's foundation office. Since many adult students are self-supporting, it is likely that every candidate will need funds sufficient to cover living expenses during the first semester. Along with financial aid dollars, funds for living expenses can be dispersed to the student on a monthly basis through the college's cashier's office. Tuition and book fees should be paid out of the scholarship and grant awards in advance of payment of any funds directly to the student. Dispersing money in this way will ensure that money intended for college expenses is not spent on other things. It will also give the student an opportunity to practice sound money management in handling personal finances. (Sources for ACP financial aid are discussed in Chapter 9.)
4. Have the candidate take a personality profile assessment and a learning styles survey. The candidate should receive immediate feedback on the results of the two tests from a trained analyst. The candidate should also receive information about how to use the results for success in the classroom and in the workplace.
5. Every ACP student should have a support team consisting of the following persons:

a. A guidance counselor/mentor—to serve as the coordinator of the support team, help to solve logistical problems, and meet with the student on a regular basis (at least twice a month)

b. A financial aid advisor—to discuss personal money management with the student. Very few financial aid advisors have the required expertise; most will require training. The college's business department can provide classes. The financial aid advisor should meet with the student at least once a month. The student should be expected to submit a log of how support dollars have been used.

c. A lead tutor—to work with other tutors in helping the student eliminate academic deficiencies. The lead tutor should keep a log of the times and dates of the student's use of tutoring services. The lead tutor should also help the student improve his or her test-taking or study skills.

Who Should Be Admitted to ACP Programs, As Determined by Formal Assessment?

Candidates who have been assessed and counseled should be grouped into three categories:

1. *Appropriate for ACP Stage 1* – This group will consist of candidates who meet the requirements for Stage 1 of the ACP program (shown in the next section). Candidates in this group will be assigned to ACP mentor/counselors who will work with them to ensure that they have:
   - Tuition/books
   - Resources for meeting personal needs
   - Resources for meeting financial needs
   - Individual development plans
2. *Require more preparation before admission to ACP* – This group will consist of students who require more than one remedial course in any core subject, along with students

who have personal problems that prevent immediate enrollment in the program.

3. *Not suitable for ACP program in the near future* – This group will consist of persons deemed by the counselor to be unsuitable for the program, due to personal problems, poor attitude, or other issues.

Criteria for Admission to the Prep Stage

Candidates who meet the following criteria should be considered suitable for admission to the Prep Stage.

1. Successfully communicates orally in English
2. Requires only limited remediation or none – No more than one course in mathematics, science, and/or English
3. Has a serious attitude about college
   - Exhibits the desire to succeed in college; is motivated by the understanding that the ACP program will lead to a rewarding career
   - Is committed to attending classes regularly and doing homework
   - Is free of addictions and is not habitually under the influence of alcohol or other drugs
   - Is open to counseling/mentoring
4. Is committed to being a full-time student for one semester
   - Has no time commitments that would preclude full-time enrollment
   - Has made arrangements for financial support
   - Has made arrangements for meeting personal needs (transportation, child care, other)

Chapter 7 Preview

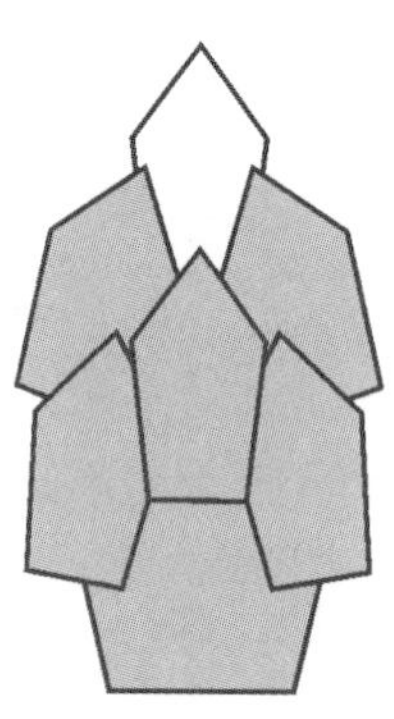

The Prep Stage (Stage 1) is the "gateway" phase of the ACP program. Successful completion of this typically 16-week, full-time college experience will enable adult students to:

- *Qualify for jobs and career ladders with participating employers,*
- *Qualify for successful educational experiences in ladder curricula, and*
- *Obtain the self-discipline and self-confidence they will need to complete the next three years of work/study and become world-class workers.*

All the pressure to succeed in the Prep Stage is not just on the ACP student; it is enormously important that the staff at the college provide the appropriate rigor and compassion to retain and mold these candidates.

This chapter outlines the structure, content, mentoring, and outcomes required in the Prep Stage.

DH & RH

THE PREP STAGE

Dan Hull

The Adult Career Pathways program offers a fresh, promising opportunity for adults to reenter education and begin rewarding careers. But to earn that opportunity, ACP students must qualify themselves by demonstrating certain abilities and personality characteristics.

The "gateway" for a student to enter and be successful in an ACP program is completion of the Prep Stage (Stage 1), a 16-to-18-week, full-time experience, offered by the college. The purpose of the Prep Stage is to enable the adult student to:

- Remove academic deficiencies and meet college entrance requirements.
- Improve personal habits, behaviors, and self-image.
- Demonstrate career interest and qualifications for employment in a career ladder.

The previous chapter presents the application and admission process for the ACP program. As that chapter points out, prospective ACP students will represent considerable diversity in educational achievements, abilities, attitudes, and personal situations. Nevertheless, despite that diversity, to be admitted into the Prep Stage, prospective ACP students should be able to demonstrate four basic characteristics:

1. *Ability to communicate orally in English*—Students with limited English proficiency should be given an opportunity to take ESL training to remove this barrier prior to admission to the ACP program.
2. *Limited need for remediation*—ACP students should enter the Prep Stage requiring no more than one course in mathematics, science, and/or English.
3. *Determination to succeed in college*—Before beginning ACP programs, prospective students should demonstrate that they:
   - Have a strong desire to succeed in their college work and understand that, apart from success in career-focused postsecondary education, their chances of obtaining employment in rewarding careers will remain slight.
   - Are committed to attend classes regularly and do homework.
   - Are free of addictions and other influences that may distract them.
   - Are open to counseling and mentoring.
4. *Willingness to commit to full-time college enrollment for one semester*—To meet this requirement, prospective students should be able to demonstrate that they:
   - Have no major time commitments that would preclude or interfere with full-time enrollment.
   - Have made adequate arrangements for financial support for tuition, books, and living expenses.
   - Have made adequate arrangements to meet their personal needs (transportation, child care, and so on).

THE PURPOSES AND STRATEGIES FOR THE PREP STAGE

The Prep Stage of the ACP program is designed to help the adult student in three areas:

1. *Improvement in career focus, self-confidence, and study skills*—In general, one of the main reasons prospective ACP students are career-limited is that they have encountered barriers to academic success. As public school students, many did not give serious thought to their futures, many never learned to study, and many (for a variety of reasons) lacked the self-confidence to succeed. As a result, many (perhaps most) prospective ACP students don't really understand their own strengths and career aptitudes. To gain that understanding, most will require academic and career counseling, to include information about job opportunities in their areas of interest and what it takes to get and succeed in those jobs. Many will also require instruction, practice, and counseling to improve their study skills and self-confidence as students.
2. *Elimination of all deficiencies that would hinder admission into an AAS college ladder curriculum*—Most ACP students have a history of poor academic performance in language arts, mathematics, and/or science. CORD's experience has shown that, in many cases, the problem is not with the student but with the manner in which the student is taught. In reality, not all students learn well in conventional lecture-style settings. Within the student population as a whole, there are many learning styles. When the mode of teaching takes into consideration the diversity of student learning styles, almost all students can achieve at high levels. The key to success in this area is what is called "contextual teaching." (For more on this, see the following section.)
3. *Preparation for employment in a career ladder by a participating ACP employer*—Participating employers will be asked to hire completers of the Prep Stage. But before

they will be willing to do so, they will require assurances that the prospective employee/students have demonstrated the desire to succeed and the potential for personal growth. Completion of the Prep Stage constitutes the necessary assurance. In completing the first stage of the program, ACP students will have demonstrated that they are serious, have a definite career focus, have taken steps to alleviate personal problems that might detract from their job performance, and have attained foundational skills in their career areas.

THE ROLE OF CONTEXTUAL TEACHING IN ACP PROGRAMS

Item 2 in the previous section refers to "contextual teaching." The authors are of the firm conviction that contextual teaching is critical to the academic success of students whose learning styles do not respond well to conventional, lecture-style settings. Even in mainstream educational environments, those students usually constitute a majority—hence the expression "neglected majority" coined by contextual teaching pioneer Dale Parnell.[1]

Simply put, contextual teaching presents information "in context"—that is, in contexts that are already familiar to students and contexts that show how the information is useful outside the classroom. Contextual teaching is not about memorization of facts, definitions, and procedures. It is about motivating students to become proactively engaged in the learning process.[2] CORD,

---

[1] See Dale P. Parnell, *The Neglected Majority* (Community College Press, 1985).

[2] For an overview of contextual teaching, see Michael Crawford, *Teaching Contextually: Research, Rationale, and Techniques for Improving Student Motivation and Achievement in Mathematics and Science* (CORD, 2001). The topic is also covered in Dan Hull, *Opening Minds, Opening Doors* (CORD, 1995); Dan Hull et al., *Career Pathways: Education with a Purpose* (CORD, 2005); Dale Parnell, *Contextual Teaching Works!* (CORD, 2001); and Elaine B. Johnson, *Contextual Teaching and Learning: What It Is and Why It's Here to Stay* (Corwin Press, 2002).

a leading proponent of contextual teaching for over twenty years, recognizes five learning processes that take place when information is presented contextually. Collectively, those processes are referred to as the REACT strategy, after the acronym formed by their first letters. Following are short descriptions of the processes, along with short examples of how a teacher might encourage them.

- **R**elating—Learning in the context of one's life experiences or preexisting knowledge

  Example: Present the concept of ratios in the context of everyday situations in which substances such as fruit juices, liquid cleaners, and plant care products are mixed with water in prescribed ratios before use.

- **E**xperiencing—Learning by doing, or through exploration, discovery, and invention

  Example: Have students measure the fuel efficiency of their automobiles and determine the real cost of commuting to and from work or school over a given period of time, or of traveling to some desirable destination.

- **A**pplying—Learning by putting the concepts to use

  Example: Have students apply the concept of interest (ratios, percentages) to any number of situations involving their own money.

- **C**ooperating—Learning in the context of sharing, responding, and communicating with other learners

  Example: This process can take place in any project in which division of labor is necessary (as is normal in most employment situations). One student conducts research, another builds a display, another presents project results to the class, and so on.

- **T**ransferring—Using knowledge in a new context or novel situation—one that has not been covered in class

  Example: Have students transfer what they learned about ratios in dealing with mixtures (under "Relating" above) to the calculation of distances on a map using the map's mileage scale.

Contextual teaching reflects not only the experiences of many educators but the research of psychologists and cognitive scientists.[3] In the hands of effective teachers, contextual teaching brings creativity, enjoyment, motivation, engagement, and communication to the classroom. It eliminates the need to answer what is perhaps the most persistent of all student questions: "Why do I have to learn this?" With contextual teaching, students readily see the "why."

The need for contextual teaching in conventional classroom settings is great, but it's even greater among prospective ACP students. For any number of reasons, those adults did not "get it" the first time around. Contextual teaching offers a way for them to have second chances at academic success, which is a big part of what the ACP concept is all about.[4]

REQUIREMENTS FOR THE PREP STAGE CURRICULUM

The Prep Stage curriculum should be designed to ensure that, upon completion of the Prep Stage, the ACP student will have accomplished the following:

1. Elimination of remediation requirements
2. Development of a positive attitude toward college
    - Has more confidence and an improved self-image
    - Understands the value of completing a career-focused program of study

---

[3] See, for example, John D. Bransford, Ann L. Brown, and Rodney R. Cocking, editors, *How People Learn: Brain, Mind, Experience, and School* (National Academy Press, 1999).

[4] CORD has produced several series of contextual teaching materials. These include *Principles of Technology* (14 units), *Transitional Mathematics* (17 units in 3 volumes), *CORD Applied Mathematics* (40 units), *Applications in Biology/Chemistry* (12 units), *Physics in Context: An Integrated Approach* (2001), *Bridges to Algebra and Geometry* (2007), *Geometry* (2007), *Algebra 1* (2007), and *Algebra 2* (forthcoming). For more on these materials, contact CORD Communications, 800-231-3015, www.cordcommunications.com.

- Has the self-discipline necessary for learning

3. Identification of career goals and development of a plan to achieve them
4. Demonstrable attainment of "soft skills"
5. Demonstrable attainment of foundational knowledge and skills for the student's chosen career field
6. Demonstrable ability to use a computer and the Internet in communicating, recording data, and locating information
7. Employability in a career ladder in the student's chosen career field

A SUGGESTED CURRICULUM PLAN FOR THE PREP STAGE

Although the ACP concept is flexible enough to accommodate many variations, in general, the Prep Stage of the ACP program should involve a schedule that resembles a workweek, i.e., eight hours per day, five days per week. Students should become accustomed to arriving on time and working at least eight hours each day. Figure 7-1 shows how a student's time might be allocated during the Prep Stage.

Weeks 1–4		Weeks 5–9		Weeks 10–16	
Employability skills	20%	Career & technical skills (intro to field)	20%	Career & technical skills (intro to field)	20%
Career guidance	20%	Job entry skills (computer/Internet)	20%	Job entry skills (computer/Internet)	20%
Personal needs	20%	Career guidance	10%	Job search	10%
		Personal needs	10%	Personal needs	10%
Academic remediation (in context)	40%	Academic remediation (in context)	40%	Academic remediation (in context)	40%

Figure 7-1. Suggested Time Allocations for the Prep Stage

Within this general, flexible framework, the following points should be kept in mind.

- Academic remediation should be tailored to each student's needs. Teaching styles for the academics should be "contextual" (as described in the preceding section on contextual teaching).
- ACP students should learn a combination of general job search skills (e.g., resume writing, interviewing skills) and job search skills that are specific to the career ladders offered by the participating ACP employers for whom they are likely to work. (General career guidance materials, instruments, and programs are available in most college student services departments. Participating employers should be able to provide information on skills that are relevant to their settings.)
- Job entry skills should include keyboarding (as determined by a given career ladder) operating a personal computer, fluent use of the Internet, and use of software such as Microsoft Word, Excel, PowerPoint, and other programs that may be considered essential in the student's chosen career field.
- Career and technical skills should be broad and foundational for the chosen field. This selection should be made under the direction of an advisory committee of participating ACP employers.
- Employability skills and personal needs should include soft skills, study skills, and individual counseling. A sample syllabus is provided as the appendix to this chapter.

APPENDIX: SAMPLE SYLLABUS FOR COURSE IN SOFT SKILLS

Student Success **Fall 2006**

SLS 1101, Three Credits
MW Main Campus

Instructor:	Mrs. College Instructor	Office: L 232
Hours:	MW 8:00–9:30 A.M.	
Telephone:	(123) 456-7890	
Email:	cinstructor@ircc.edu	
Required text:	*Keys to Success, 5th ed.* by C. Carter, J. Bishop and S. L. Kravits (Prentice Hall, 2005)	
Required material:	green scantrons (6)	

Course Description
This 16-week course provides the new and returning student with special study skills proven to be effective by successful college students. New perspectives on note-taking, study skills, improved reading methods, and test taking tactics, are presented to the students through lecture, multimedia, internet activities, guided modeling, and individual and group activities. These new tools generate greater self-confidence and the ability to view learning as a natural part of the thinking process.

Attendance
Attendance is critical for success in any venture and therefore is important to the successful completion of this course. Only two absences will be allowed before a two-point reduction from the attendance points will occur for each absence. Tardies after the scheduled start of class or leaving prior to the scheduled end of class will result in a one-point deduction. Students with no tardies and no absences will earn 15 bonus points added directly to their semester total.

Requirements—Students will be called upon to participate, both formally and informally, in instructor-guided class discussions during the semester. This participation will help students to prepare for a well-planned, pre-scheduled, oral presentation. A script must be submitted on the day of presentation.

Each student will write 5 compositions in the form of reaction writings. Students will choose their topics from a list supplied by the instructor. Each written reaction will be a minimum of three paragraphs. Please see the writing handout for more detailed instructions.

Every student must take the final exam at the end of the term in order to receive a final grade.

Students are expected to complete all assigned activities.

Last day to withdraw from the course with a "W" is Nov. 15, 2006.

Grading—Following is the point system, and scale, by which all grades are determined.

Attendance	100 points	A = 630–700
Reaction Writings	100 points	B = 560–629
Oral presentation	100 points	C = 490–559
Activities	100 points	D = 420–489
Tests	200 points	F = 419–below
Final exam	100 points	

Make-up work is allowed only at the discretion of the instructor. Any missed test that the instructor allows to be made up will be done in the last week of the semester.

There are opportunities for bonus points for additional assignments.

Please refer to the "day by day syllabus" at least every other day. It contains detailed course content and assignments with the due dates.

Course Topics

Defining Yourself

Appreciating diversity

Reviewing and using the IRCC catalog

Becoming motivated and staying that way

Discovering your learning styles and knowing which study methods are best suited to your style

Setting goals from the perspective of individual values

Linking goals with time, values, and priorities

Scheduling strategies and beating procrastination

Mastering Student Skills

Thinking critically:
- problem solving
- challenging assumptions
- the role of creativity

Becoming a better reader:
- Dealing with overload and distractions
- SQ3R: a method for reading academic material

Note-taking:
- Three different patterns
- How to write faster

Becoming an effective writer

Listening as a skill

Test-taking strategies

Creating the Successful Life

Communicating effectively:
- Styles of communication
- Body language

Learning relationship strategies

Dealing with conflict and criticism

Maintaining personal wellness:
- Exercise: aerobic, strength, balance and flexibility
- Stress management
- Alcohol, tobacco, and drug abuse
- Sexual decisions information

Mapping a career path:
- Money plans
- Safe spending
- Student credit cards

Dealing with the reality of change and unpredictability

Handling success and failure

Giving back to the world

Living with integrity

Chapter 8 Preview

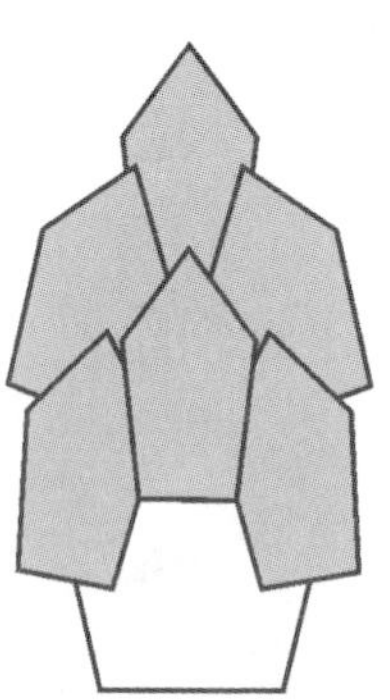

Combining good education with good job training is a tricky challenge. And combining education and training with career-progression within an employer organization is even more difficult. Educators must understand employer requirements at each stage, and integrate them with the appropriate scope and sequence of the ladder curriculum. Employers must design a career ladder that fits the needs of the workplace with a sequence of rewards and job progression that are compatible with student-employee success. The process is difficult, but achievable; successful models are shown in the healthcare field.

DH & RH

CAREER LADDERS AND LADDER CURRICULA

Bonnie Rinard and Holly Doughty

Remember Karla from the Prologue? When we last encountered Karla, she was a 24-year-old single parent who had barely graduated from high school. Like far too many young people, she was waiting tables and had to live with her parents because her job didn't provide enough for her to support herself and her child. Karla was frustrated. She wanted a "real" career, but she didn't know how to get it, and she was tied down by her responsibilities as a parent.

Karla applied for an entry-level job at a local telecommunication company but was not considered because she didn't have the required education and experience in the field. The interviewer in the company's human resources department suggested that she inquire about the new Career Pathways program at the nearby community college.

After several false starts, Karla finally got up the nerve to meet with the college's ACP Counselor. Karla learned that several telecommunication companies were working together with the college to offer a three-year "work and learn" program for adults like her. After a few sessions and some testing, the counselor determined that Karla would be eligible for admission to the program if she would complete a 16-week, full-time Prep Stage to prepare her for entry-level employment and admission to an associate degree program. To do this, Karla had to quit her job waiting tables. The college counselor arranged *for Karla to receive tuition, childcare, transportation, and a stipend of $1000 a month to cover living expenses during the 16-week Prep Stage.*

During the Prep Stage, Karla met frequently with the ACP Counselor, who encouraged her and helped her to work through academic and personal problems. By the time she had completed the Prep Stage she had eliminated her academic deficiencies in math and English, learned effective study skills, and achieved a level of self-confidence and self-discipline that she had never before experienced. Better still, as she became acquainted with the telecommunication industry – something she had previously known almost nothing about – she found that a "high-tech" career appealed to her very much. For the first time in her life, she was setting her sights on a long-term goal, something she really wanted and could be proud of. Armed with the entry-level knowledge and technical skills she had gained during the Prep Stage, Karla was offered a part-time job at a participating telecommunication company. While working there 30 hours a week, she took nine credit hours in the college's IT program. Karla had officially entered Stage 2 of her ACP program.

Karla learned that her job was the first of nine rungs on the company's "career ladder." She could advance to the next rung by completing the Stage 2 coursework at the college (one semester, 9 credit hours) while maintaining satisfactory job performance. At that point she would become a full-time employee with benefits and tuition reimbursement. From then on, she could advance through the rungs of the ladder by continuing part-time study at the college, one semester per rung. Karla was assigned an "employee mentor" who helped her navigate her job assignments and deal with job-related or personal problems.

At last Karla was one her way to something good, and she was loving it.

CLIMBING THE CAREER LADDER

The ACP concept is founded on an approach to curriculum and career preparation in which the student/employee progresses through a series of steps, like rungs on a ladder. Hence the terms *career ladder* and *ladder curriculum*.

A career ladder is a series of steps or occupational levels within a given company or occupation. Employees work their way up career ladders by increasing their knowledge and skills and contributing to the success of the companies for which they work. In most cases, each rung entails a higher level of responsibility than the one(s) below it, along with higher pay and/or other benefits. Whether, and how fast, a person advances along a career ladder is determined by his or her ability to meet *standards,* specific requirements as to what the person must know and be able to do before moving up. Some standards are developed locally by individual companies, others by government agencies, professional associations, or advisory boards that oversee entire industries.

In an Adult Career Pathway, cooperating employers—some of whom might normally be competitors—develop a common career ladder that is applied consistently among the ACP students who work for those employers.

WHAT IS A LADDER CURRICULUM?

Just as a career ladder denotes a series of job-performance levels, each corresponding to certain knowledge and skills within a given occupational area, a *ladder curriculum* consists of a series of educational levels that students are expected to attain as they move through their programs. When the programs are career-focused, as is the case with ACP, the knowledge and skills to be mastered through the ladder curriculum should be determined *jointly* by educators and employers. Employers are uniquely qualified to say what employees in their fields should know and be able to do. By definition, every ACP curriculum advisory committee should include representatives of the employers for whom the ACP students will work. (Examples of ladder curricula are provided as Appendices 8-1, 8-2, and 8-3.)

RATIONALE FOR CAREER LADDERS AND LADDER CURRICULA IN ACP PROGRAMS

The ladder curriculum model is flexible enough to meet the needs of a wide range of students, including students within the target populations of this initiative. Most ladder curriculum programs are designed to be "doable," that is, they present the student with numerous attainable intermediate goals with frequent rewards and multiple exit and reentry points. Because of personal difficulties, ACP students may sometimes need to exit their ACP programs temporarily to work full time. Ladder curricula typically accommodate that need by giving students some kind of marketable skill at each level and enabling them to reenter their programs at a later time.

The ladder curriculum approach represents a win-win proposition that offers benefits to both students and employers.

Benefits of Ladder Curricula

To students

- Structured yet flexible
- Attainable short-term goals
- Clear goals and procedures
- Mutual commitment
- Increased opportunities
- Student satisfaction

To employers

- Greater worker productivity
- Increased employee retention
- Increased base of skilled employees
- Mutual commitment
- Access to employees with varying skill levels
- Opportunity to impact curriculum
- Employer satisfaction

Benefits for Students

The ladder curriculum model is structured yet flexible. It presents the student with numerous short-term goals that are within easy reach and provide occasions for positive reinforcement. Criteria for progress are clearly stated, along with the procedures involved in reaching program goals, so student/employees don't have to guess at how well they are doing. When ladder curricula are well established and clearly understood by all parties concerned, advancement in education and employment is perceived as attainable. When student/employees think of themselves as "climbing a ladder" to long-term success, rather than merely putting in time, they are more likely to be high producers and take pride in their work. Whereas many workplace environments are adversarial, ladder curriculum programs create environments in which student-employees and employers are mutually committed to one another's success.

Benefits for Employers

Employers benefit in several ways from the mutual commitment fostered by curriculum ladder programs. Probably the greatest is increased employee retention. When student-employees enjoy what they do, and perceive that their employers take a genuine interest in their well-being, they are far more likely to stay with those employers over time—saving the costs associated with employee retraining. A ladder curriculum program gives employers a prospective employee base that is not only large but diverse in its skill levels. Ladder programs also ensure that employers don't have to expend large amounts of time and money training graduates of their area schools. In ladder curriculum programs, employers are encouraged—in fact, expected—to play a major role in selecting standards and determining the content of the career education programs in those schools.

THE DESIGN PROCESS FOR CREATING A LADDER CURRICULUM

Ladder Curriculum Design

There is no standard template for creating a ladder curriculum. Because of its flexibility, the ladder curriculum model can be custom fitted to different settings. In some cases, it might not take the form of a ladder—in which students progress in a strictly linear fashion—but rather a lattice or web, allowing for lateral movement as well. Not all students are able to work through their educational programs sequentially without stopping. Some make lateral moves, exiting their programs to take care of personal needs, work full time, or acquire additional knowledge and skills appropriate to their current levels before progressing to the next levels.

It is important to note that, even though on-the job learning (via internships or similar arrangements) is an essential component of the ladder curriculum model, credentialing constraints limit the amount of internship credit that can be counted toward degree completion. In the generic model presented at the end of this chapter, we have placed the internship credits in the last stages of the program, to allow for the tailoring of the curriculum to meet the specific needs of the employer.

The number of levels in the program will depend on the certification(s) or degree to be awarded. (A typical AAS curriculum requires 60 credit hours, or nine ACP stages after the Prep Stage.) As stated above, successful transition from each stage to the next is contingent on completion of required coursework and job performance (if the student is beyond the Prep Stage).

As with Career Pathways in general, the structural design for the *curriculum framework* of the ACP should include the following three levels:[1]

- *Foundational level*—Contextual academics, career experiences, and basic work skills
- *Technical core level*—Technical skills within a cluster and work-based learning opportunities
- *Technical specialty level*—Advanced technical skills, advanced academics, and worksite experiences

---

[1] In this context, a curriculum framework is a *plan* for an ACP. Curriculum frameworks consist of two elements: (1) recommended course sequences and (2) course descriptions, with prerequisites, recommended grade levels, credits, and standards to be achieved by students. For more, see Chapter 3 of Dan Hull et el., *Career Pathways: Education with a Purpose* (CORD, 2005).

Career Pathways/Career Clusters

The structure of an ACP will always differ from that of a conventional grade-9–14 Career Pathway.[2] Whereas grade-9–14 Career Pathways give students three or more years of high school to explore careers and acquire soft skills and basic technical skills, the adult learner in an ACP program must cover the same territory in one semester (the Prep Stage). Another key difference has to do with focus. Grade-9–14 Career Pathways are intentionally broad so that students' options remain open, especially while they are still in high school. Even at the conclusion of grade 14 (the associate degree), the student is prepared not so much for a specific job but for a range of jobs within a cluster. With ACP, on the other hand, the student begins very early to focus on specific jobs, and even specific employers.

Principles and Agreements That Should Underlie the Ladder Curriculum

The following principles and agreements should be acknowledged and in place before beginning the development of the ladder curriculum:

- The participating employers should agree on *one* career ladder and how each part of the curriculum will correspond to each rung of the ladder. (This issue is discussed in Chapter 5.)
- The employers should agree on the minimum requirements for job entry. (Students take steps to meet these requirements in the Prep Stage.)
- The employers should agree not to lure ACP students away from other participating employers.
- If possible, the career ladder curriculum should culminate in an associate degree, to ensure transferability of employee credentials.

---

[2] See Hull et al., Chapter 3.

- The participating employers must agree to support the general education requirements of the Prep Stage. (One purpose of the ACP concept is to encourage students to plan for the long haul. They should not be encouraged in any way to settle for less than an associate degree or comparable credential.)
- Entrance to Stage 2 should be contingent upon the student's having cleared all academic deficiencies.
- To help employers realize a return on their investment, students should be encouraged to continue working for their employer sponsors after completion of their programs.

Who Is Involved?

The curriculum committee should be composed of two groups: (1) representatives of the local businesses that will employ the ACP students and (2) community college personnel (especially faculty members) who will work with the program's students. The business representatives should be middle managers who understand the jobs that the ACP student-employees will perform and who understand the organization's long-term vision and overall trends in their industry. Community college representatives could be department heads and faculty members from the career clusters being developed. Everyone on the curriculum committee should be open, flexible, and dedicated to working for the good of the students.

Key Steps in the Ladder Curriculum Development Process

Identify Appropriate Skill Standards

Selection— The curriculum committee should gather all available skill standards pertaining to the career cluster being addressed. These will consist of three general types: academic, employability, and technical. Standards have been published by numerous entities at multiple levels (national, regional, industry, and academia).[3]

Review—The employers on the curriculum committee should review cluster skill standards and tailor them to local needs. If national skill standards do not exist, the employers will have to develop their own, focusing not only on the knowledge, skills, and attitudes required for entry-level employment in their industries, but on the requirements for upward mobility along the career ladder in their local areas. Employment levels and the criteria for promotion will naturally vary from company to company. But by committing to the ACP program, employers are agreeing to seek a compromise that all parties can accept.

Identify Certifications and Degrees That Are Attainable at Different ACP Stages

The curriculum committee should identify and agree on the certifications, licenses, and/or degrees that the ACP curriculum would qualify students to receive. This would also involve correlating each ACP stage to the appropriate award or credential. (For most stages, there may be no certificate, license, or degree, but the completion of every stage should be formally acknowledged in some way.) If, for a given pathway, there are relatively few industry certifications to award, the committee should create its own certificates of achievement to be awarded as students are promoted from each stage to the next. This will help to keep students motivated. Employer incentives such as pay increases, additional job duties, and progressive job titles should also be considered.

Create a Sequenced or Tiered List of Standards

Published standards must usually be tailored to the local specifics of the ACP program to which they are being applied. This process involves matching, or sequencing, the elements of the standards to the requirements for the various certification,

---

[3] See, for example, the numerous publications of the Electronics Technicians of America (http://www.eta-i.org/Study.html).

licensure, and degree options that the ACP program offers. This may mean breaking down and resequencing some elements of the standards. The overall result of this process will be a customized list of standards that moves from generalities to details and applies specifically to the ACP program under consideration. The last few stages of the curriculum ladder might include employer-specific standards.

Select and/or Create Courses

When the list of standards has been compiled, the next step is to select and/or create courses that prepare students to meet those standards. (Of course, the participating educational institutions' requirements for graduation and the awarding of degrees and certifications must also be considered and woven into the ACP curriculum.) The courses should be sequenced in such a way that, in progressing from each ACP stage to the next, students build on previously acquired knowledge and are able to satisfy the career-ladder requirements of the participating employers. While the tendency might be to put off the general education requirements until the later stages, we recommend that these be taken care of early. (Again, the purpose of the ACP is to help students embark on and complete a long-term process that will serve them throughout their lives. If students are allowed to skip general education requirements in pursuit of some low-level certification, their long-term interests are not well served.)

The methodology and pedagogy used in teaching these courses should be tailored to the needs of the students, most of whom do not respond well to conventional, lecture-style teaching environments. The authors strongly recommend contextual teaching, as described in Chapter 7.

Plan Where the Standards Will Be Addressed in the Courses

The curriculum committee should next determine which courses will address which standards. If existing courses are used, it will usually be necessary to recombine, tailor, or otherwise alter the courses to meet the standards mandated for the program. Each course should have a detailed outline. The outlines should clearly identify how each standard will be addressed in each course. For example, the committee may determine that the *communication* standards should be addressed in all courses, along with some of the employability standards such as *teamwork* and *dealing with diversity*. While the importance of those standards may be obvious to the committee, the topics will not be given sufficient emphasis in the classroom unless the instructor and the students see an explicit requirement in the course outline. The outline should state course requirements in detail rather than generally. For example, instead of a general statement such as, "Students will complete a project," the outline should provide detailed statements such as this:

> Working in small groups, students will complete a project. Afterward students will prepare a report (written or oral depending on communication skills that are being emphasized). In addition, each student will write a paragraph describing the group dynamics in working on the project and how the group could improve its performance in the future.

The added specificity emphasizes the need to address communication and teamwork skills in conjunction with academic skills.

Develop Assessment Strategy and Tools

The standards drive student assessments, how progress is measured, and the effectiveness of the educational process. Assessment tools and instruments should be developed to determine whether students are progressing appropriately. Assessment tools could include rubrics, checklists, pencil-and-paper tests, portfolios, on-demand demonstrations, and structured observations. Given the dual role of ACP students as both students and employees, assessments should cover not only coursework but job performance. To ensure standardization in the assessment process, the people involved in the evaluation of the student/employees should be trained to administer assessments.

Determine Logistics for Course Delivery

Determine when and where courses will be offered and whether special facilities are required. Explore multiple delivery methods and identify the ones that provide the best mix for the audience and locale. More and colleges are offering multiple class delivery methods, including online delivery. Options for ACP courses might include distance learning, worksite classes, online courses, extended semesters, unique scheduling, internships, and others. Given ACP students' need for flexibility in scheduling, exploration of alternate delivery methods should be considered essential.

Alternate strategies for course delivery—The proposed structure for ladder curricula in ACP programs places heavy demand on student-employees' time during Stages 3–10. ACP student-employees are typically required to take 6–9 credit hours each stage (semester), while working full time. We are suggesting that participating employers provide up to ten hours of paid release time per week for ACP participants. Alternative delivery strategies should also be considered, such as the following:

- Teach courses at employer facilities, assuming that there is a "critical mass" of students at the site.
- Consider coordinating work assignments with course content. This creates an internship-like experience.
- Design courses in such a way that the classroom portion is taken "online," leaving only the labs, or practica, to be conducted at the college. This strategy is increasingly popular among colleges that provide courses for working adults.

Identify Resources to Be Used

The curriculum committee should compile a list of texts, websites, and other resources that support the teaching and learning of the relevant content.

Ongoing Support of the Ladder Curriculum

Ladder curricula require regular maintenance and fine-tuning. The curriculum committee should meet periodically throughout the curriculum implementation process to ensure that the curriculum is accomplishing its purpose. Changes and adjustments should be made accordingly, bearing in mind that the curriculum is designed to meet the needs of both students and their employers, and to satisfy requirements established by the college.

APPENDIX 8-1: GENERAL LADDER CURRICULUM MODEL

The following is a general ladder curriculum model that could be applied in any Career Pathway. The model includes the three skills levels referred to above (foundational, technical core, and technical specialty).

The certifications cited are only examples. In practice, the intermediate levels of attainment would differ from model to model. The ultimate goal of every ladder should be an associate degree.

The prescribed schedules for working hours and course load, beginning in Stage 2, may be overly ambitious for some adult students with family responsibilities. A more realistic schedule for some would be:

- 20 hours/week part-time work in Stage 2
- 30 hours/week full-time work in Stages 3–10 (This assumes that employers would give ACP students paid release time, up to 10 hours/week, to attend classes.)

1) **Stage 1:** One semester, full-time student[4]
2) **Stage 2:** Part-time student (9 cr hr), part-time employee (30 hr)
   a) Entry-level academics: Remediation requirements should have been eliminated in the Prep Stage
   b) Entry-level skills (to include soft skills)
   c) *Developmental technical core*
   d) *Foundation class* (general education requirement)
3) **Stage 3:** Part-time student (6 cr hr), full-time employee
   a) *Developmental technical core*
   b) *Foundation class* (general education requirement)

   Certificate attainment: Employability at level A[5]
4) **Stage 4:** Part-time student (6 cr hr), full-time employee
   a) *Intermediate technical core*
   b) *Foundation class* (general education requirement)

   Certificate attainment: Employability at level B
5) **Stage 5:** Part-time student (6 cr hr), full-time employee
   a) *Intermediate technical core*
   b) *Foundation class* (general education requirement)

   Certificate attainment: Employability at level C
6) **Stage 6:** Part-time student (6 cr hr), full-time employee
   a) *Intermediate technical core*

   Certificate attainment: Employability at level D
7) **Stage 7:** Part-time student (6 cr hr), full-time employee
   a) *Technical specialty*

   Certificate attainment: Employability at level E
8) **Stage 8:** Part-time student (6 cr hr), full-time employee
   a) *Technical specialty*

---

[4] For more complete information on what Stage 1 (the Prep Stage) entails, see Chapter 7.

[5] Employment levels A, B, C, and so on are arbitrary. They are intended merely to indicate that the student-employee is making forward progress at his or her place of employment.

9) **Stage 9:** Part-time student (6 cr hr), full-time employee
    a) *Technical specialty*
    b) Industry/occupation Internship credits
10) **Stage 10:** Part-time student (6 cr hr), full-time employee
    a) *Technical specialty*

Certificate attainment: Employability at level F
Degree attainment: Associate

APPENDIX 8-2: SPECIFIC LADDER CURRICULUM MODEL

Following is a model for a career ladder in computer programming, along with the corresponding ladder curriculum. Students who perform the coursework outlined in the model should qualify for industry certifications in computer information systems and degree attainment (A.A.S degree in computer programming) as indicated at the corresponding stages in the ladder.

It is important to note that this model represents a specific progression through certification levels. Every model will show variations in levels of certification and the lengths of study necessary to attain certifications and degrees.

Computer Programming Career Ladder

Programmer/Analyst I (A+ Certification)
Programmer/Analyst II (Network+ Certification)
Programmer/Analyst III/Lead programmer (Certified Netware Administrator)
System Analyst/Manager (Microsoft Certified Professional)
System Administrator/Engineer (Microsoft Certified Systems Engineer)

Computer Programming Ladder Curriculum (Specific)

1) **Stage 1:** One semester full-time student
2) **Stage 2:** Part-time student (9 cr hr), part-time employee (20–30 hr/wk)
   a) Microcomputer applications
   b) Programming fundamentals I
   c) English-composition
3) **Stage 3:** Part-time student (6 cr hr), full-time employee
   a) Programming fundamentals II
   b) A+ training
   c) English-technical/business writing

   Certificate attainment: A+ certification
4) **Stage 4:** Part-time student (6 cr hr), full-time employee
   a) Introduction to programming/operating systems
   b) Network+ training (elective credit)
   c) Mathematics

   Certificate attainment: A+ certification/ Network+ certification
5) **Stage 5:** Part-time student (6 cr hr), full-time employee
   a) NetWare administration
   b) Programming/operating systems
   c) Natural sciences/social behavioral science

   Certificate attainment: CNA certification
6) **Stage 6:** Part-time student (6 cr hr), full-time employee
   a) Programming/operating systems (supporting servers/MCP[6] required class)
   b) Programming/operating systems (web programming I)

   Certificate attainment: College certificate in programming
7) **Stage 7:** Part-time student (6 cr hr), full-time employee
   Programming/operating systems (Visual BASIC)
   Programming/operating systems (web programming II)

   Certificate attainment: MCP certification

---

[6] Microsoft Certified Professional

8) **Stage 8:** Part-time student (6 cr hr), full-time employee
   a) Programming/operating systems (database programming)
   b) Programming/operating systems (programming III)
9) **Stage 9:** Part-time student (6 cr hr), full-time employee
   a) Programming/operating systems (advanced programming)
   b) Programming/operating systems (computer organization and language)
10) **Stage 10:** Part-time student (6 cr hr), full-time employee
    a) Programming/operating systems (tech security)
    b) Industry/occupation internship credits (internship)

Certificate attainment: MCSE[7] certification
Degree attainment: A.A.S. in programming

[7] Microsoft Certified Systems Engineer

APPENDIX 8-3: OTHER EXAMPLES OF LADDER CURRICULA

Ladder curricula, linked to career ladders, are already in place at some community colleges, particularly in the field of nursing and patient care. Following are examples from Lansing Community College in Lansing, Michigan, and Muskegon Community College in Muskegon, Michigan.

Career Ladder Nursing Program, Lansing Community College

The Career Ladder Nursing Program is composed of the Practical Nursing (PN) Program and the Associate Degree Nursing (ADN) Program (Curriculum Code for both programs is 0863).

The PN PROGRAM is approved by the Michigan Board of Nursing (since November 1970). The program consists of 21–25 semester credits of general education requirements and 23 semester credits of nursing course requirements. These courses provide the basis for an in-depth study of the theory and nursing care of adults, children and families. Clinical experiences include extended-care facilities, hospitals, and community agencies where students provide nursing care to geriatric, medical, surgical, maternity, and pediatric patients.

Graduates earn certificates from Lansing Community College and are eligible to take the National Council Licensing Examination–Practical Nurse (NCLEX-PN). Those who pass the examination are entitled to practice as Licensed Practical Nurses (LPNs).

The ADN PROGRAM is approved by the Michigan Board of Nursing and is accredited by the National League for Nursing Accrediting Commission (NLNAC, Inc., 61 Broadway-33rd Floor, New York, NY 10006; 212/363-5555; www.nlnac.org). LCC's nursing program has had continuous accreditation since 1971. The program consists of the PN Program described above with an additional 9–11 semester credits of general education requirements and 21 semester credits of nursing courses.

These courses provide the basis for an in-depth study of the theory and nursing care of children, adults, and families. Clinical experiences include hospitals, home health care agencies, rehabilitation units, and community health organizations where students provide nursing care to mental health, medical, surgical, maternity, and pediatric patients. Students are responsible for applying beginning leadership skills in supervising members of the health team. Student learning experiences progress from simple to complex and use critical thinking skills in applying the nursing process to the care of patients. Graduates earn AAS degrees from Lansing Community College and are eligible to take the National Council Licensing Examination—Registered Nurse (NCLEX-RN). Those who pass the examination are entitled to practice as Registered Nurses (RNs).

Alternative Part-Time Format

The Career Ladder Nursing Program Alternative Format for Part-Time Students within Lansing Community College's Nursing Department will enable the nontraditional student to pursue a terminal degree (Associate Degree in Applied Science) in nursing while maintaining their existing life responsibilities. This program is an innovative community initiative that addresses the critical shortage of registered nurses.

Some of the courses are offered in a Hybrid format, meaning that students will be required to meet face-to-face with their instructor and also complete coursework online. For hybrid learning information click here.

Thirty-two students will be admitted each fall semester. Coursework will consist of theory, labs and clinical rotations. The program will be eight consecutive semesters in length; sixteen weeks during the fall and spring, and eight weeks in the summer.

The successful graduate will be eligible to write the NCLEX-RN Exam with subsequent Registered Nurse licensure in the State of Michigan.

Adapted from the website of Lansing Community College (http://www.lcc.edu/nursing/nursing/index.htm).

Nursing Career Ladder, Muskegon Community College, Muskegon, Michigan

Level II—RN				**ASSOCIATE IN SCIENCE AND ARTS DEGREE**		Total 84 cr
	Term 7 15 wk	ENG	102	English Composition	3 cr	
				Western World Cultures Group	3 cr	
				American Culture Elective	3 cr	Transfer degree
				Aesthetic Values Elective	3 cr	
				ASSOCIATE IN APPLIED SCIENCE DEGREE		Total 72 cr (20 non-nursing)
	Term 6 15 wk	NUR	222A	Managing the Care of the Family	5 cr	
		NUR	211A	Care of the Family in Psychological Crisis	4 cr	
		ANTH	103	Cultural Diversity in Contemporary Society	3 cr	
	Term 5 15 wk	NUR	212B	Care of the Family in Physiological Crisis	8 cr	
		BIOL	207	Microbiology	3 cr	
				Coreq: BIOL 207A Lab	1 cr	
				Prereq: BIOL 105		
Level I—PN				**PRACTICAL NURSING DIPLOMA**		Total 37 cr (11 non-nursing)
	Term 4 15 wk	NUR	141B	Care of the Maturing Family	8 cr	
		PHIL	204	Biomedical Ethics	3 cr	
		PEA		PE Activity or Dance Elective	1 cr	
	Term 3 15 wk	NUR	131B	Care of the Childrearing Family	8 cr	
		BIOL	106	Anatomy & Physiology II	4 cr	
	Term 2 15 wk	NUR	125	Basic Physical Assessment	1 cr	
		NUR	124A	Care of the Childbearing Family	4 cr	
		NUR	123A	Intro. to Nursing Practice	3 cr	
		NUR	121	Environmental Stressors and Pharmacotherapeutics	1 cr	
		ENG	101	English Composition	3 cr	
	Term 1 15 wk	NUR	100	Overview of the Nursing Profession	1 cr	
		AH	111	Environmental Stressors and Nutrition	1 cr	
		BIOL	105	Anatomy and Physiology I	4 cr	
		COM	100	Principles of Communication	1 cr	
		PEA	101A	Fitness, Wellness, and Nutrition	1 cr	
		PSYC	201	General Psychology	4 cr	
				ENTRY LEVEL COMPETENCIES		
	Entry level	GRADE	10	Reading Level		
		ENG	091	Intro. to English Composition		
		CIS	100	Intro. to Personal Computers		
		CSS	100	College Success Seminar		
		MATH	035 or 036	Basic Mathematics		

Adapted from the website of Muskegon Community College (http://www.muskegoncc.edu/pages/572.asp)

Resources

Chapter 9 Preview

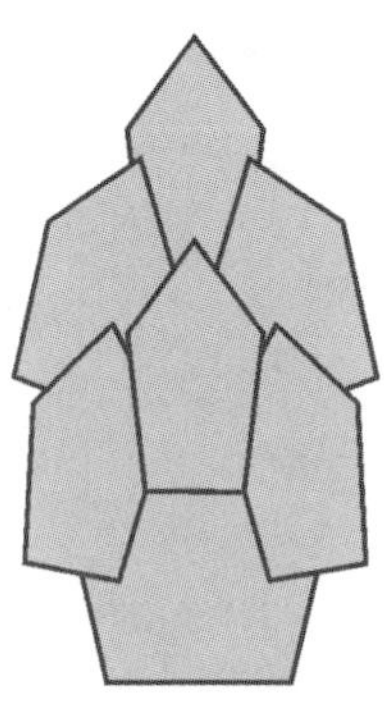

In most communities, funding to partially support adult students attending community colleges seems to be adequate. This is a false assumption, for two reasons:

- *Most adult students are working and taking one or two courses per semester. Very few of these part-time students ever complete full programs of study.*
- *Only a very small percentage of adults who need a two-year college education are enrolled.*

When the ACP vision, as presented in this book, is fully adopted in each community, there will not be sufficient federal, state, and local funds to support the students. Hopefully, new and different, coordinated policies will be enacted to alleviate the shortfalls, but substantial support from the private sector (participating employers who will benefit from an improved workforce) will have to be realized.

This chapter identifies the cost elements of ACP programs, provides a framework for developing budgets, and suggests the relative magnitude of support from each source (federal, state, local, community/faith-based organizations, and employers.)

DH & RH

WHO FOOTS THE BILL?

Frank Jennings and Dan Hull

Every community in the United States has adult residents who are not economically self-sufficient, either because they are not working or because they are working at jobs that cannot lift them and their families above the poverty line. The needs of those people do not go unnoticed. Community and technical colleges work hard to provide programs that are accessible to low-income adults, as do institutions such as one-stop career centers and area technical education centers. Many community and faith-based organizations consider meeting the needs of the poor to be one of their highest priorities.

If we were to put a dollar figure on the amount of money—public and private—spent to improve the lives of the less fortunate in this country over the past half-century, what would it be? Of course, that's an unanswerable question, but certainly the amount would run into many billions. The obvious next question is this: Has it worked? Has all that money and time and effort helped America's low-income families rise to a level at which they no longer need public assistance? For some families, the answer is yes. Every assistance program has its success stories. But all around us we still see large numbers of frustrated adults who fall far short of their potential, and the problem seems to be getting worse rather than better. Clearly, as a nation, we still have not arrived at an effective solution.

Here are three of the main reasons why (in our view) a comprehensive solution has not been found:

- Most intervention strategies are designed to provide a "quick fix" rather than solve the underlying problem. They relieve the symptoms (temporarily) but do not cure the patient. While the strategies called for in this book are difficult and expensive, we believe those strategies could produce life-changing experiences for many people.
- Existing efforts are largely uncoordinated with one another. Many agencies across the country offer basic education, assistance in meeting personal needs, and career training, but they are not systematically coordinated or aligned. The result is excessive red tape, confusion, and duplication of effort.
- There are simply not enough federal and state financial resources available to address the magnitude of the problem, which is huge and growing.

Although the cost of implementing the ACP strategy proposed in this book is high, the cost of *not* implementing it will ultimately be much higher. As unemployment (and underemployment) rise, so does the cost to taxpayers for welfare and incarcerations. And the shortage of well-trained workers severely limits economic development, causing more and more of America's wealth to be transferred abroad.

Subsequent chapters identify the revenue available from existing federal, state, and local sources, as well as new policies called for by the proposed plan of action. This chapter focuses on identifying the specific cost elements of ACP programs and provides a general strategy for meeting those costs. The proposed strategy calls for a significant investment, especially on the part of businesses, but also promises a strong return in the form of loyal, well-qualified employees who add value to their employers' products and services and support themselves and their families without the need for public assistance.

WHAT ARE THE ACP COST ELEMENTS?

ACP candidates represent a wide range of backgrounds, resources, and needs. At one end of the spectrum will be people who need little or no remediation and have access to at least *some* form of support, such as the GI Bill, the income of working spouses, or other family support. At the other end will be people—far more numerous—who represent "worst-case scenarios," for example, single parents with serious personal and academic needs but no support whatsoever. In the following paragraphs, in laying out the costs of ACP programs, we use "worst-case scenario" assumptions as a kind of baseline. If ACP programs are to succeed, they must be prepared to help people whose needs are great. Programs that set their admission standards too high will fail to reach the very people who need the programs most urgently and stand to gain the most through participation.

We do not provide a comprehensive, specific budget. Budgets must be developed locally, taking into consideration the availability of resources (public and private) and the willingness of employers and community organizations to participate. What follows here is a *budget template* that covers nine elements:

1. Program planning, design, and development
2. Student recruitment and intake
3. Counseling and mentoring
4. Tuition, teaching materials, and supplies
5. Living costs
6. Transportation
7. Childcare
8. Paid release time to attend classes
9. Other ACP cost elements

While the actual costs incurred for each of these elements will differ from one program to the next, every program's budget will have to cover all nine to some extent.

Let's look at the nine elements in detail.

1. *Program planning, design, and development*—This element represents a one-time cost, although budgeting for it should also take into consideration the need for periodic

program evaluation and revision. Planning, design, and development include the time and effort required to form partnerships and negotiate agreements. (This process will probably require the services of independent consultants.) The planning process will also involve activities such as visits to sites where aspects of the ACP concept are already working; research into program designs and materials; meetings; and development and/or acquisition of materials and faculty training that support teaching, recruitment, and counseling. Program staff should be hired well in advance of the program's first day of operation.

2. *Student recruitment and intake*—This element involves materials and activities designed to give the program visibility. They will include marketing pieces (printed and online), staff time for presentations to potential supporters, publications in newspapers and periodicals, telephone calls, and visits to community and faith-based organizations and individuals.

   Intake of applicants requires experienced personnel who have the expertise to design application materials, select and acquire test and assessment instruments, screen applicants, administer and evaluate assessments, interview applicants, arrange for financial and other assistance, and schedule classes. Recruitment and intake tasks are ongoing, or recurring costs. (Further details on recruitment and intake are provided in Chapter 6.)

3. *Counseling and mentoring* – Most ACP students will require counseling (individual and group) both prior to their admission to and during their participation in the program. During Stage 1, counseling and mentoring should take place at least weekly. As the student moves through the stages, counseling by college staff members will be required less frequently.

   Career counseling, provided during Stage 1, will include administration and evaluation of student aptitude and interest assessments. In conjunction with that process, counselors will also help students identify and learn about the high-demand jobs that are within their reach. (Where possible, counselors should seek opportunities for students to visit worksites.)

Part of the counseling role will fall to employee mentors. Most community and technical colleges are equipped to provide the necessary preparatory training to the mentors. Participating employers should look upon the cost of the mentors' time as part of their contribution to the success of the programs.

Counseling and mentoring represent recurring costs. (Further details on counseling and mentoring are provided in Chapters 6 and 7.)

4. *Tuition, teaching materials, and supplies* – The cost of administering classes will be determined by the college and factored into student tuition. Tuition, teaching materials (student texts and workbooks), and supplies (expendables) will be provided through the college for Stage 1. In subsequent stages, these costs will be borne by the student and/or the employer.
5. *Living costs* – During Stage 1, students will attend classes full-time. This means that, for the most part, the students and their dependents will need help in paying their living expenses (meals, clothing, medical expenses, and so on). Some colleges have externally funded programs that can provide food and clothing for students who qualify for assistance. During Stage 2, students will be employed part-time and thus be able to meet at least part of their own living expenses. After Stage 2, the students will be full-time employees and should be able to support themselves and their families.
6. *Transportation* – Some ACP students will require help with transportation in getting to and from classes. If they live near public transportation arteries, the costs will be limited to fares charged by the carriers. If they live in places where public transportation is not readily available, other arrangements will have to be made.

Community and faith-based organizations could be called upon to provide assistance in this area.

7. *Childcare* – At least 30 percent of ACP students will require childcare. This could be arranged through the colleges, some of which provide childcare in special circumstance, or with the assistance of community and faith-based organizations. This element represents a high priority. One reason many adults are fearful of going back to school is that they have small children and cannot afford childcare. ACP programs should be equipped to provide or arrange for childcare during times when students are attending classes or fulfilling other responsibilities that specifically pertain to their participation in the program. The greatest need for help with childcare will occur during Stage 1, when the students attend classes full-time. Childcare could be provided by community and faith-based organizations or purchased from for-profit daycare centers. Childcare costs can range from $250 to over $800 per month, depending on the children's ages and how many hours per week they are in care.
8. *Paid release time for ACP employees to attend classes*— Beginning with Stage 2, ACP student-employees work and attend classes at the same time. To make this possible without excessive hardship on the student, we recommend that employers be willing to provide paid release time of one or two hours a day for their ACP student-employees to attend classes. This represents a real cost to the employers, but we believe that, in the long run, that cost will be repaid several times over.
9. *Other ACP cost elements*— As stated at the beginning of this section, the preceding items represent only a *template* for determining and meeting ACP program costs. The specifics will vary from place to place, from program to program, and even from one student to the next. The essential point is that program planners and administrators be thorough in making provisions for all possible costs. Any potential barrier to participation,

however small it might seem, could exclude the very people whom the ACP concept is designed to help.

ESTIMATING AND ALLOCATING THE COSTS

The cost elements identified in the previous section are deliberately general, with no dollar amounts or percentages assigned. Assignment of numbers to the elements will take place on a *local* basis, as determined by the infrastructure and general circumstances in a particular setting. Using the framework shown in Table 9-1, the numbers can then be assembled into a detailed ACP budget.

The table leaves the "estimated cost" column blank because costs will vary by locality and program. One of the ACP coordinator's first jobs is to determine what numbers will go in each space. The table also leaves extra space under *Source(s) of funds*. Here again, the items that fall under that category will vary. (Chapters 10–12 describe current policies and funding sources at the federal, state, and local levels. These chapters also provide recommendations for new policies that would focus more succinctly on ACP issues and provide adequate funds to support them.)

In our discussions with community leaders about the feasibility of ACP programs, we have noted that adequate funds seem to be available already. The problem is not lack of funds, but that a pitifully small percentage of the adults who so urgently need ACP have been recruited into adult education programs of any kind! In most instances, the biggest reason for low enrollment in career preparation programs for adults is lack of employer involvement. The promise of good jobs with career ladders is the strongest motivator for unemployed and underemployed adults who want to improve their status in life. When employers don't make an effort to help struggling adults see the connection between education and rewarding careers, those adults see no reason to go back to school. (Chapter 6 speaks to the recruitment problem and suggests effective strategies for recruiting, enrolling, and retaining ACP students.)

Table 9-1. Allocation of Costs for ACP

Cost element	Est. cost	Occurs when?	Services provided by	Source(s) of funds
Planning, design, training, and development (*one-time cost*)		Before program begins	College, employers, comm. leaders and consultant	Community Capital Campaign
Recruitment and intake		Before Stage 1	College	Existing college programs and ACP staff
Counseling and mentoring		Before Stage 1	College	Existing college programs and ACP staff
		During Stage 1	College	
		During Stage 2	College and employer	Existing college programs and individual employer
		Stages 3–10	Employer	Individual employer
Tuition, teaching materials, and supplies		Stage 1	College	Federal, state and community
		Stages 2–10	College and employer	Federal, state and employer
Student/family living costs/ Transportation		Stage 1	Combination of tuition assistance programs, community-based organizations and community capital campaign	Federal, state and community
		Stages 2–3		Federal, state, community, employer and student
		Stage 4–10	Combination of student earnings, employer support, community based organizations	
Childcare		Stages 1–10	College and/or community	Community
Paid release time to attend classes		Stages 2–10	Employer	Employer

A PROPOSED STRATEGY FOR SHARING ACP COSTS

Well-populated ACP programs are needed in virtually every community in this country. However, if the vision presented in this book were to become a reality, the numbers of ACP programs and students would soon outstrip the availability of federal, state, and local funds to support them. A much larger share of the costs would have to be borne by employers. In this section we present a strategy for sharing the costs of ACP programs.

The proposed funding strategy calls for a large commitment from employers. Specifically, the employer partners for each ACP program would be asked to do the following:

1. Participate in the planning phase of the program by partnering with competitor organizations to create a common career ladder for intake and growth of new employees.
2. In collaboration with other employers in the same cluster (including competitors), agree on a common set of entry-level knowledge, skills, and personal qualities for new employees.
3. Hire ACP students after they have completed the first stage of the program.
4. Provide one or more mentors for each newly hired ACP student-employee, to work with that student-employee for two to three years.
5. Provide incentives for completion of each ACP stage.
6. Support ACP student-employees by providing health insurance, tuition, and books for all courses above Stage 1, where appropriate, offer paid release time of a few hours a week to make it easier for ACP student-employees to attend classes.

Figure 9-1 shows how employers' contributions would relate to support acquired through other sources. Table 9-2 provides sample figures for an average ACP student-employee.

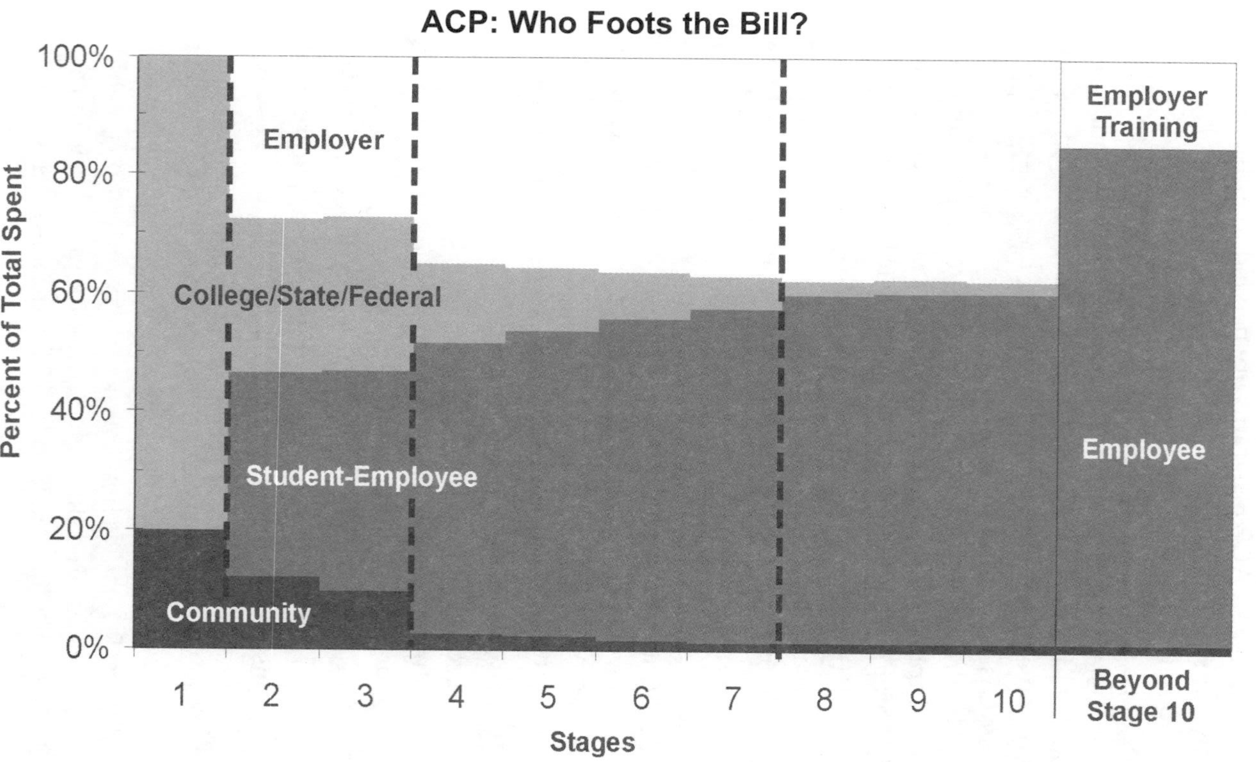

Figure 9-1. Support Cost Allocations for Average ACP Student-Employee

Table 9-2. Cost Breakdown for Average ACP Student-Employee

Assumptions: Medium living expenses; each stage represents four months; student is single parent; all $ amounts are pretax; overall goal is for program graduate to be qualified for $16/hour full-time job

Stage	**1**	**2**	**3**	**4**	**5**	**6**	**7**	**8**	**9**	**10**	**Totals**
Hours of Instruction	12 NC; 3 CR	9	6	6	6	6	6	6	6	6	60
Paid release (Hours/Week)	—	5	5	10	10	10	10	10	10	10	
Hours of Work/Week	—	30	30	40	40	40	40	40	40	40	
Pay Rate		8.00	8.50	9.00	9.50	10.00	10.50	11.00	11.50	12.00	
Use of Funds											
Tuition, fees, and books	1,800	1,080	1,080	720	720	720	720	720	720	720	7,200
Student family living costs	4,000	4,000	4,000	4,000	4,000	4,000	4,000	4,000	4,300	4,475	36,775
Health Insurance	2,000	2,000	2,000	2,000	2,000	2,000	2,000	2,000	2,000	2,000	18,000
Transportation	600	600	600	600	600	600	600	600	600	600	5,400
Social Security and inc. tax	—	400	425	600	633	667	700	733	767	800	5,775
Childcare	1,600	1,600	1,600	1,600	1,600	1,600	1,600	1,600	1,600	1,600	14,400
	***10,000**	9,680	9,705	9,520	9,553	9,587	9,620	9,653	9,987	10,195	****87,500**
Source of Funds											
Student-employee earnings	—	3,333	3,613	4,650	4,908	5,167	5,425	5,683	5,942	6,200	44,921
Paid release time	—	667	638	1,350	1,425	1,500	1,575	1,650	1,725	1,800	12,329
Employer benefits (health)	—	2,000	2,000	2,000	2,000	2,000	2,000	2,000	2,000	2,000	18,000
College/state/federal	8,000	2,500	2,500	1,250	1,000	750	500	220	220	195	9,135
Community	2,000	1,180	955	270	220	170	120	100	100	—	3,115
	***10,000**	9,680	9,705	9,520	9,553	9,587	9,620	9,653	9,987	10,195	****87,500**

*Total cost for Prep Stage; **Total cost of program

In reviewing Figure 9-1 and Table 9-2, bear in mind the following:

- In Stage 1, ACP students attend college full-time. They are almost completely dependent on support from the program for their tuition, books and supplies, and living expenses. Funds to support this stage will come from various sources. Most ACP students will be eligible for Pell Grants, Federal SEOG Grants, and State Public Education Grants. Colleges can provide information on grants, scholarships, and subsidized loans.
- Following successful completion of Stage 1, ACP students are hired by participating employers and placed in career ladders.
- In Stages 2 and 3, ACP students take a total of 15 course hours at their colleges in the prescribed ladder curricula. During these stages, the students work 30 hours per week and are given five hours of paid release time per week. The employer provides health insurance as an additional benefit.
- In Stages 4–10, ACP students are full-time employees on a graduating pay scale. They are able to meet increasing percentages of their own living expenses. They continue to take six credit hours per semester in their ladder curricula. The employer increases the paid release time to 10 hours per week.
- By the end of Stage 10 (approximately three years), ACP students have completed their ladder curricula and are financially independent. Employer-sponsored training may be provided for advanced skills.
- Support from community and faith-based organizations should be available for childcare, general living expenses, and transportation until students are fully independent.

The example in Table 9-2 would require the employer to commit just over $30,000 for release time and health benefits over three years.

ACP programs will vary in duration, content, schedule, and modes of support. The plan proposed in this chapter is not intended to be prescriptive or to call for strict replication. Its purpose is to help ACP planners identify major cost elements, provide a framework for budgets, suggest trends in funding, and set the stage for the chapters on federal, state, and community policies.

Chapter 10 Preview

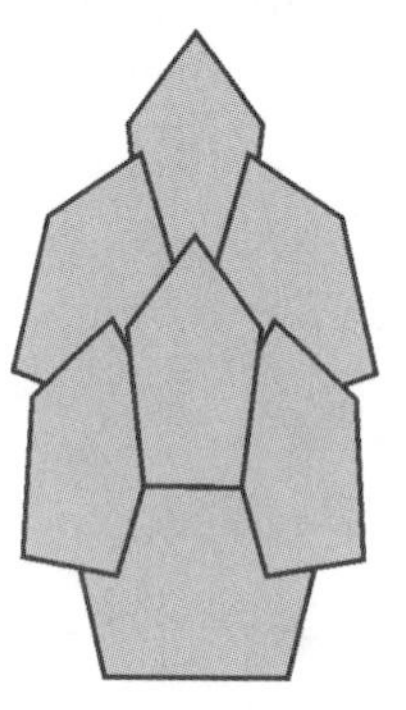

There's a lot of federal money available to support elements of ACP programs – if you can only find it. Despite several major efforts, in the last 35 years, to overhaul and streamline programs for workforce development and jobs for the needy, the bureaucracy of federal guidelines continues to mask these sources from those who need them. ACP coordinators and their staff will have to search out these sources and make them available to ACP students.

This chapter is a compilation and description of federal programs with funding streams that may provide resources for ACP elements. Some of these programs are directed for youth; persons over 24 years old are not eligible recipients.

The chapter also points to the need for specific policies to assist adults in ACP programs.

DH & RH

Federal Policies and Programs to Support Adult Career Pathways

Michael Brustein and David Bond

I. Introduction

This chapter sets out a roadmap to help the reader navigate the larger federal programs (and some smaller ones) that could provide support for Adult Career Pathways (ACP). We provide only brief summaries. The summaries include references to more comprehensive information about the programs. Since these federal programs are state-administered, we recommend that the reader access both the state and local plans and applications. It is very important to understand the dynamics at the federal, state, and local levels to effectively access resources to support ACP.

As stated in the previous chapter, the most assistance is needed in Stage 1, when the individual is a full-time student. In later stages, the student (now a student-employee) becomes more self-sufficient while progressing into part-time then full-time employment—climbing the career ladder. Those who begin at minimum wage have a deep hole from which to climb. Fortunately, Congress is addressing this.

According to the National Center on Education and the Economy, the primary purpose of adult basic education and publicly funded job training is to get poor people into the workforce as soon as possible. Because this has been the case, the adult basic education and job training system has been largely disconnected from public policies and institutions designed to promote local and regional economic development. In many highly industrialized countries, the adult basic education system is intended to enable a much larger fraction of the adult population to achieve much higher education standards.[1]

If other countries provide better access to specialized training than the United States, we should not be surprised to find out that the foundation skills and knowledge of our workers are well below those of our competitors. The literacy of American workers, compared to workers in other countries, is mediocre. According to Willard Daggett, President of the International Center for Leadership in Education, entry-level workers in technical fields need higher-level literacy skills than management due to the technical manuals that entry-level workers must master.[2] The federal government should be concerned about adult literacy and technical training if the United States is to stay ahead of our economic competitors. American schools, according to the Organization for Economic Cooperation and Development, are well funded relative to the schools in other advanced industrial nations, but this country's public job training system is not, relative to the job training systems in the countries with which we compete.[3]

---

[1] National Center on Education and the Economy (NCEE), *Tough Choices or Tough Times: The Report of the New commission on the Skills of the American Workforce* (Jossey-Bass, San Francisco, 2007).

[2] Willard R. Daggett, "Preparing Students for the 21st Century Workplace: The Need for Partnerships" (presentation delivered at the Texas Business and Education Coalition's 11th annual VIP briefing, February 2, 2007).

[3] NCEE, *Tough Choices or Tough Times.*

II. HISTORY

According to MDRC, efforts to promote work among welfare recipients began almost 40 years ago. At first, federal funding was limited, participation in employment and training activities was voluntary, and programs mostly targeted recipients of Aid to Families with Dependent Children (AFDC) who had no preschool children.[4]

Writing from a historical perspective, John Wallace, in *A Vision for the Future of the Workforce Investment System*, made the following four observations:

1. From the 1960s, the workforce system's mainstream programs for adults were designed to move unemployed, low-income people—including unemployed, dislocated workers—into work or reemployment through a range of preemployment services. By and large, job retention and job advancement services—including retraining programs for currently working people—were not part of the services menu for workforce development programs. The workforce system's target population and services were entirely appropriate—until perhaps ten years ago.
2. Only in the last few years has the system worked more closely with employers.
3. The workforce system has, by and large, kept its distance from the other major public job preparation program in the country, namely, the one run by welfare agencies for welfare recipients. It is also notable that most workforce agencies played little role in promoting receipt of two major work supports administered through the tax system—the Earned Income Tax Credit (EITC) and Child Tax Credit (CTC).
4. When the main goal of the workforce system was to move unemployed people into work, it was appropriate to have performance standards that focused on the employment outcomes of program participants. The

---

[4] *MDRC's Evolving Welfare Research Agenda, 2007* (http://www.mdrc.org/area_issue_12.html; accessed January 17, 2007).

> performance standards became—and continue to be—powerful drivers of the entire system. But there is increasing evidence that the current performance standards may well have had the unintended consequence of driving the system in the wrong direction. In attempting to meet or exceed the standards, programs may have enrolled and placed many people who would have found training or jobs on their own.[5]

The **Comprehensive Employment and Training Act** (or **CETA**, Pub. L. 93-203) is a United States federal law enacted in 1973 to train workers and provide them with jobs in the public service. The program offered work to those with low incomes and the long-term unemployed as well as summer jobs to low-income high school students. Full-time jobs were provided for a period of 12 to 24 months in public agencies or private not-for-profit organizations. The intent was to impart marketable skills that would allow participants to move into unsubsidized jobs. It was an extension of the **Works Progress Administration** program from the **1930s**. CETA was intended to decentralize control of federally controlled job training programs, giving more power to the individual state governments. Nine years later, it was replaced by the **Job Training Partnership Act**.

The Job Training Partnership Act of 1983 was designed to improve the employment status of disadvantaged young adults, dislocated workers, and individuals facing barriers to employment. Program components include on-the-job training, job search assistance, basic education, work experience, and improving participants' occupational skills. The 1998 Workforce Investment Act replaced JTPA.

MDRC states that in the 1980s, states began to require some recipients to participate in work activities, and the federal government began to provide more funding for employment services and supports like childcare subsidies. By the mid-1990s, most states were expanding work requirements to a broader segment of the caseload and experimenting with more radical

---

[5] John Wallace, *A Vision for the Future of the Workforce Investment System* (MDRC, January 2007).

measures, such as time limits on benefit receipt and "full family sanctions" —penalties that close a family's entire welfare case when the adult fails to participate in work activities without good cause. States also took steps to "make work pay" by allowing recipients to keep more of their benefits after going to work. This experimentation culminated in the 1996 federal welfare law, which eliminated the AFDC program and created, in its place, the Temporary Assistance for Needy Families (TANF) block grant. TANF was reauthorized by Congress in early 2006. For more on TANF, see the section entitled "Current Programs."[6]

Congress attempted with limited success to simplify the maze of federal categorical programs that target career education for adults when it passed the Workforce Investment Act (WIA) in 1998 (29 U.S.C. 2801 et seq.[7]). The intent behind this reform piece of legislation was to consolidate the scores of separate employment and training programs and offer adults a "no wrong door approach" to career training. The 1998 WIA created a "one-stop" system, whereby every local workforce area in the nation was required to bring the business, education, and labor communities together to provide universal access to training for adults in a one-stop environment. The 110th Congress is expected to streamline these efforts even further.

III. CURRENT PROGRAMS

The largest programs are administered through the Departments of Education, Labor, and Health and Human Services, but other federal agencies continue to administer smaller programs that target adults in need of a second chance in education.

This section lists several of the major programs and ends with a group of programs for "out-of-school" youth. The table provided as the appendix to this chapter gives some brief summary information (funding, purpose, target population) for

---

[6] *MDRC's Evolving Welfare Research Agenda 2007.*

[7] This statute is available at: http://frwebgate.access.gpo.gov/cgi-bin/getdoc.cgi?dbname=105_cong_public_laws&docid=f:publ220.105.

the major programs described, along with a few smaller programs.

The Workforce Investment Act

The largest source of federal funding to support adult workforce education is the Workforce Investment Act (WIA) (29 U.S.C. 2801 et seq.[8]). Title I of the WIA is "Workforce Investment Systems." It contains three separate funding streams to cover programs for economically disadvantaged youth, adults, and dislocated workers. The youth program is currently funded at $940 million, the adult employment and training program is funded at $857 million, and the dislocated worker program is funded at $1.58 billion. The three funding streams are administered by the Employment and Training Administration within the U.S. Department of Labor.

Although WIA funds are federal, the funds are awarded through each state's Office of the Governor. The Governor is responsible for the creation of each state's workforce investment system. The Governor appoints a state Workforce Investment Board that advises the Governor on the designation of local workforce areas and the establishment of a local workforce board for each area. The chief elected officials in each workforce area appoint members to the local boards. The majority of the board must be from the private sector. The interests of adult education and postsecondary career technical education are represented on these local boards. Each local board is required to establish a one-stop delivery system to meet the needs of both consumers and local employers. There are over 650 of these workforce areas across the United States. The operation of the one-stop system is governed by a memorandum of understanding among nearly 20 one-stop partners that represent a variety of federal training programs.

The federal funds that are available for adult employment and training are administered through the one-stop operators.

---

[8] This statute is available at: http://frwebgate.access.gpo.gov/cgi-bin/getdoc.cgi?dbname=105_cong_public_laws&docid=f:publ220.105.

Services available through the one-stop system are offered in three tiers:

- Core services
- Intensive services
- Training services

Eligibility for intensive services requires that the adult was first provided with core services. Eligibility for training requires that the adult has received both core and intensive services.

Core services include information, outreach, and assessments to help adults find jobs, know what skills and training are required for those jobs, and locate providers. All providers must be certified by the one-stop operator. Consumers are given relevant information on the providers' placement rates. On the basis of this information, adults can make informed choices as to where to seek training.

Intensive services are designed for the unemployed and those who are unable to obtain employment through core services or those who are employed but need intensive services to retain employment that leads to self-sufficiency. Intensive services include comprehensive and specialized assessments, diagnostic testing, counseling, career planning, and prevocational services.

Adults who are unable to secure employment after receiving core services and intensive services, and dislocated workers, are eligible for *training services.* Dislocated workers are individuals who have been terminated or laid off and are unlikely to return to their former jobs. Adults eligible for training services under the WIA select the training provider. Training services include occupational skills training, on-the-job training, cooperative education programs, skill upgrading and retention, entrepreneurial training, job readiness training, adult basic education and literacy training, and customized job training. The training is provided through the use of individual training accounts or vouchers. As long as the adult pursues training through a provider on the local board's approved list, the one-stop operator will process the voucher to assist in the payment for services. The training accounts are need based and are made available with other funding sources such as Pell grants.

The statute identifies a select list of programs that are required to partner with the workforce system for the delivery of services through the One-Stops, in an effort to build comprehensive workforce development systems across the country. WIA Partner Programs include adult education programs for individuals with limited basic skills or English language skills; Trade Adjustment Assistance (TAA) for trade-impacted dislocated workers; the Employment Service responsible for labor exchange and administration of unemployment insurance systems; Vocation Rehabilitation for individual with disabilities; Older Worker Community Service Employment; Postsecondary Vocational and Technical Education; and Employment and Training programs provided through the Community Service Block Grant, and federal Housing Acts. WIA also encourages (but does not require) partnering with other programs including: Welfare reform (TANF); Food Stamps Employment and Training; and National and Community Service Employment programs.[9]

As mentioned above, the WIA was an attempt by Congress to streamline federal categorical programs that target adult career pathways. In addition, according to Mary Gardner Clagett, WIA was intended to fundamentally change the way workforce development services were provided across the United States through pursuit of the following objectives:

- Consolidation of programs, streamlining of services, and coordination of remaining workforce programs;
- Transfer of authority for system design and implementation to States and especially to local areas;
- Establishment of high-level, business-led state and local workforce boards, responsible for the design and oversight of workforce investment systems;

---

[9] Mary Gardner Clagett, "Workforce Development in the United States: An Overview" (paper prepared for the *New* Commission on the Skills of the American Workforce, National Center on Education and the Economy, October 2006).

- Development of an easily accessible, comprehensive One Stop system for the delivery of employment and training services;
- Development of a voucher-like mechanism (Individual Training Accounts) for accessing training;
- Establishment of a demand-driven system, meeting the economic development and business needs of state and local workforce areas—recognizing two equally important customers—job seekers and employers;
- A strengthened performance measurement system, requiring continuous improvement and holding state and local workforce systems accountable for employment-related measures, including customer satisfaction.[10]

The Adult Education and Family Literacy Act (AEFLA)

In 1998, Congress consolidated several smaller adult education and literacy programs under Title II of the WIA and entitled it "The Adult Education and Family Literacy Act" (20 U.S.C. 9201 et seq.[11]). The AEFLA is administered by the U.S. Department of Education. It is currently funded at $563 million, of which $68 million must be expended on programs in English language and civics; these funds are allocated by the Secretary to state eligible agencies for instruction below the postsecondary level. These state agencies allocate the funds as grants or contracts on a competitive basis to eligible providers. The target populations are individuals who have attained the age of 16, are not enrolled or required to be enrolled in secondary school, and who lack sufficient mastery of basic educational skills to enable them to function effectively in society.

AEFLA funds create a partnership among the federal government, states, and localities to provide adult education and literacy services to (1) assist adults to become literate and obtain

---

[10] Clagett, "Workforce Development in the United States."

[11] This statute is available at: http://frwebgate.access.gpo.gov/cgi-bin/getdoc.cgi?dbname=105_cong_public_laws&docid=f:publ220.105.

the knowledge and skills necessary for employment and self-sufficiency, (2) assist adults who are parents to obtain the educational skills necessary to become full partners in the educational development of their children, and (3) assist adults in the completion of secondary school education. This is the largest federal program whose primary purpose is to promote adult literacy. While the priority is targeted to functional literacy, some states and locales use AEFLA funds to prepare adult populations for the GED.

Eligible providers of these services include local educational agencies, community-based organizations, volunteer literacy organizations, institutions of higher education, public or private nonprofit agencies, libraries, and public housing authorities. These providers must submit an application to the State eligible agency. The application must describe how the funds will be spent, but the focus must be on literacy training. Although the AEFLA is expected to be rewritten this year, we do not expect substantive change to this structure.

The Carl D. Perkins Career and Technical Education Act of 2006 (Perkins IV)

Although earlier versions of the Vocational Education Act, particularly the original 1963 Act and the Amendments in 1968, 1976, and 1984, targeted assistance for adult career education, that support has been dramatically circumscribed by the more recent reauthorizations of Perkins. The most recent Congressional action, the Carl D. Perkins Career and Technical Education Act of 2006 (Perkins IV) (20 U.S.C. 2301 et seq.[12]), supports the development of academic and career and technical skills of secondary and postsecondary students who elect to enroll in career and technical education (CTE). CTE is defined as organized educational activities that offer a *sequence* of courses that provides individuals with coherent and rigorous content aligned with challenging academic standards, and relevant

---

[12] This statute is available at: http://frwebgate.access.gpo.gov/cgi-bin/getdoc.cgi?dbname=109_cong_bills&docid=f:s250enr.txt.pdf.

technical knowledge and skills, needed to prepare for further education and careers in current or emerging professions. The focus of Perkins IV is on "first chance" students rather than adults in need of a second chance in education.

Perkins IV has specifically dropped its prior references to serving the academically disadvantaged and high school dropouts. The new law prohibits the use of funds in any respect for remedial courses. Congress was determined to navigate a new course for the Perkins Program, giving greater emphasis to academic rigor.

Despite this change in direction, some states still look to Perkins as a source of support for adult workforce training, particularly at the community college level. Many high school completers as well as non-completers pursue career training at the community college level. These postsecondary institutions are eligible to receive Perkins funds, but the burden rests with the institution to use the funds only to serve CTE students. These adult students must be enrolled in articulated sequences of courses that lead to technical skill proficiency, industry-recognized credentials, certificates, or associate degrees. Each CTE adult student's progress would then have to be assessed in accord with the stringent accountability requirements in Perkins IV. Resources are not available under Perkins to support adult education, where the emphasis is on literacy.

To the extent that community and technical colleges are serving these adult populations in CTE programs, they are eligible to submit applications to the State for Perkins funds. Similar to the AEFLA, Perkins IV is state-administered. The Secretary of Education awards approximately $1.3 billion annually to the states for Perkins and Tech Prep programs. The states, in turn, individually determine how much to allocate for secondary and postsecondary programs. Once that split is made, the state must allocate the funds to eligible recipients based on a formula determined by Congress. The Perkins Statute is prescriptive on the matter of allowable uses of funds.

Temporary Assistance to Needy Families (TANF)

TANF was created by Congress in 1996 to eliminate the open-ended entitlement of welfare (42 U.S.C. 601 et seq.[13]). Administered by the Department of Health and Human Services, the Act provides (through block grants to states) time-limited cash assistance to needy families so that children can be cared for in their own homes. The focus of the legislation is to promote job preparation and work.

States are given the flexibility to determine eligibility for benefits and the method of assistance. However, they must maintain their own contributions to TANF; the nonfederal contribution is 80 percent. The program is currently funded at approximately $17 billion.

Most of the TANF dollars are allocated by formulas to local social service agencies. Since this is a "Work First" program, basic skills education is limited to a fraction of a client's 30-hour work requirement. Some states have defined vocational education training to include basic skills instruction.

The Federal Pell Grant Program

The Federal Pell Grant Program, funded at approximately $13.6 billion (*with up to $4 billion more based on the number of eligible students*), was first enacted as Part A, Subpart 1 of Title IV of the Higher Education Act of 1965 (20 U.S.C. 1070a[14]). Most recently the program was reauthorized and amended by the 1998 Reauthorization of the Higher Education Act (HEA). The Pell Grant Program provides need-based grants to low-income undergraduate and certain post-baccalaureate students to promote access to postsecondary education. Students can use their grants at any one of approximately 5400 participating postsecondary institutions. Under certain circumstances,

---

[13] This statute is available at: http://www.access.gpo.gov/uscode/title42/chapter7_subchapteriv_.html.

[14] This statute is available at: http://www.law.cornell.edu/uscode/html/uscode20/usc_sec_20_00001070---a000-.html.

students can receive two Pell Grants, but cannot receive funds from more than one school at a time.

Eligibility for a Pell Grant is dependent on the student's expected family contribution (EFC), the cost of attendance (as determined by the institution), the student's enrollment status (full-time or part-time), and whether the student attends for a full academic year or less. The fundamental elements in determining the EFC are the student's income (and assets if the student is independent), the parents' income and assets (if the student is dependent), the family's household size, and the number of family members (excluding parents) attending postsecondary institutions. The EFC is the sum of: (1) a percentage of net income (remaining income after subtracting allowances for basic living expenses and taxes) and (2) a percentage of net assets (assets remaining after subtracting an asset protection allowance). Different assessment rates and allowances are used for dependent students, independent students without dependents, and independent students with dependents. Pell Grant awards differ based upon all of these factors.

Students who qualify for need-based aid can also receive loans on which interest rates are lower and repayment is deferred due to federal subsidies. The federal government also guarantees some loans for students who do not demonstrate financial need.

The Montgomery GI Bill

The GI Bill was originally enacted under The Servicemembers' Readjustment Act of 1944 and ended in July 1956. In 1984, the program was reenacted as the All-Volunteer Force Educational Assistance Program, commonly known as the Montgomery GI Bill, after former Mississippi Congressman Gillespie V. "Sonny" Montgomery (38 U.S.C. 3001 et seq.[15]). The Montgomery GI Bill, funded at approximately $192 million, established two new

[15] This statute is available at: http://www.law.cornell.edu/uscode/html/uscode38/usc_sup_01_38_10_III_20_30.html.

educational programs: an assistance program for veterans who enter active duty after July 1, 1985 (with some additional eligibility for veterans with past service); and an assistance program for certain members of the Selected Reserve. The main purpose of the program is to assist in the readjustment of members of the Armed Forces to civilian life after their separation from military service and to extend the benefits of a higher education to qualifying men and women who might not otherwise be able to afford this education. Its other primary purpose is to establish a program of educational assistance based on service on active duty or a combination of service on active duty and in the Selected Reserve, including the National Guard, to aid in the recruitment and retention of highly qualified personnel for both the active and reserve components of the Armed Forces.

The Montgomery GI Bill for active-duty service members, referred to as MGIB, provides up to 36 months of education benefits to eligible veterans for various training programs, including college, technical or vocational courses, correspondence courses, apprenticeship or job training, flight or high-tech training, licensing and certification tests, entrepreneurship training, and certain entrance examinations. Veterans are eligible if they: (1) have been honorably discharged from the armed forces; (2) have high school diplomas or GEDs (or in some cases 12 hours of college credit); and (3) meet specified combinations of requirements (determining placement in specified "categories"), which include start date of active duty, length of service, and amount contributed to the program. While enrolled in one of the educational programs listed above, eligible veterans receive a monthly benefit based on the type of training program, length of service, and applicable category. For most veterans, the time limit for using the MGIB benefits is ten years, but in certain circumstances, the time limit can be less.

The Montgomery GI Bill for members of the Selected Reserve (Army Reserve, Navy Reserve, Air Force Reserve, Marine Corps Reserve and Coast Guard Reserve, and the Army National Guard and the Air National Guard), referred to as MGIB-SR, provides up to 36 months of education benefits to eligible members. The educational benefits can be used for degree programs, certificate or correspondence courses, cooperative training, independent study programs, apprenticeships and on-the-job training, vocational flight training programs, and remedial, refresher and deficiency training (under certain circumstances). Generally, reservists are eligible for benefits if they: (1) have a six-year obligation to serve in the Selected Reserve signed after June 30, 1985 (officers must have agreed to serve six years in addition to their original obligation); (2) complete their initial active duty for training (IADT); (3) have a high school diploma or equivalency certificate before completing IADT; and (4) remain in good standing while serving in an active Selected Reserve unit. Reservists whose eligibility for this program began on or after October 1, 1992, have 14 years from the beginning date of their eligibility, or until the day they leave the Selected Reserve, whichever is later, to use their MGIB-SR benefits. Reservists whose eligibility began prior to October 1, 1992, have 10 years, or until the day they leave the Selected Reserve, whichever is later, to use their MGIB-SR benefits.

Jobs-Plus

The Jobs-Plus Community Revitalization Initiative for Public Housing Families (Jobs-Plus) program was sponsored by a consortium of public and private funders led by the U.S. Department of Housing and Urban Development and the Rockefeller Foundation. The initiative had three core components: employment-related services and activities; financial incentives to work; and community support for work. An MDRC report titled *Promoting Work in Public Housing: The Effectiveness of Jobs-Plus, Final Report, Executive Summary* (2005) evaluated and described how the program operated as a special demonstration project in selected housing developments in six U.S. cities.[16]

---

[16] H. S. Bloom, J. A. Riccio, and N. Verma, *Promoting Work in Public Housing: The Effectiveness of Jobs-Plus* (MDRC, 2005). http://www.mdrc.org/publications/405/full.pdf. Accessed January 17, 2007.

MDRC's report indicated that, across all six sites combined, the program increased residents' average annual earnings by 6.2 percent beyond what they would have been without the program. In sites where the program was implemented well, the earnings increase averaged 14 percent. The demonstration suggested that an employment-focused intervention based in public housing developments can work. The initiative provides a promising approach for helping individuals achieve self-sufficiency through current workforce law.

Programs for Out-of-School Youth

Although some programs such as Job Corps, YouthBuild, and Youth Service and Conservation Corps begin serving youth at age 16, eligibility for some extends to age 24 or 25, which is at the beginning of the adult spectrum under consideration.

Martin and Halperin (2006) described several programs that either have or had federal funding, before being turned over to the states.[17] Some of these programs (Opportunities Industrialization Centers and YouthBuild) began as private programs in large cities, or in individual states, and then received federal funding in order to spread these successful programs to other cities and states. A list of these programs is as follows:

- **Job Corps**—The Economic Opportunity Act of 1964 ("The War on Poverty") established the Job Corps. Today, Title I-C of the WIA authorizes the program. About 65,000 young people enroll each year. The majority (88 percent) of Job Corps sites are residential, such that students live at the center while enrolled. The programs for 16- to 24-year-olds employ a comprehensive career training and youth development approach, combining academic, vocational, and employability skills; social competencies through classroom instruction; community service; hands-on practical

[17] Nancy Martin and Samuel Halperin, *Whatever It Takes: How Twelve Communities Are Reconnecting Out-of-School Youth* (American Youth Policy Forum, Washington, DC, 2006).

learning environments; and support services to prepare youth for employment and responsible citizenship. Congress appropriated $1.56 billion for Job Corps for FY 2006.

- **Opportunities Industrialization Centers** – OIC has been moving people from poverty and welfare to self-sufficiency, employment, and empowerment for over 41 years. Founded by the late Reverend Dr. Leon H. Sullivan in 1964, OIC had its origins in the civil rights movement, the War on Poverty, and the urban unrest of the 1960s when Sullivan rallied 400 ministers in Philadelphia to create employment opportunities for low-income residents in the inner city. Since that time, OIC has grown to 33 states and the District of Columbia. It is funded by corporate contributions and federal grants from the U.S. Departments of Labor, Health and Human Services, and Justice. OIC's philosophy of developing the whole person involves life skills development, fundamental education, job skills training, and employment readiness services. Over 40 percent of OIC's students are dropouts.
- **YouthBuild** – YouthBuild was founded in 1978 by Dorothy Stoneman in East Harlem. In this program, unemployed and undereducated young people, ages 16 to 24, work towards completion of a GED or high school diploma while learning work and social skills by building affordable housing for homeless and low-income people. The programs emphasize leadership development, community service, and the creation of a positive community of adults and youth committed to success. In 2004, there were more than 200 programs in 44 states, engaging approximately 7,000 young adults annually. It is a public-private partnership, currently funded about 50 percent from the Federal government, 35 percent from foundation, 9 percent from corporations, and 6 percent from donations. Federal support is authorized under Subtitle D of Title IV of the 1992 Cranston-Gonzalez National Affordable Housing Act. In FY 2004, the U.S. Department of Housing and Urban Development awarded $54 million in grants to 93 local YouthBuild programs.

- **Youth Service and Conservation Corps** – These are nonprofit programs that engage youth and young adults (ages 16 to 25) in full-time community service, training, and education. Since the late 1950s, the U.S. federal government has experimented with comparatively large investments in a Youth Conservation Corps and a Young Adult Conservation Corps, the latter enjoying an annual budget of about $260 million. The Reagan administration ended such efforts and the youth corps torch was passed to the states. The modern corps are state and local programs that do not enjoy a dedicated source of federal funds.

IV. PROBLEMS/CHALLENGES

While there have been some success stories across the nation, the nature of bureaucracy is such that adults in need of a second chance are still subjected to a conflicting array of program offerings. Despite numerous attempts over the past ten years to streamline federal efforts to provide support to enable career-limited adults to enter the workforce, we still witness a "patchwork" of federal job training programs for adults. These programs still retain conflicting rules and administrative structures, so there is no simple explanation for accessing or understanding the federal programs that support adult career education.

Besides the complexity of this issue, federal investments in second-chance education and training programs fell from $15 billion in the late 1970s to $3 billion (inflation-adjusted) today.[18] Currently, the workforce investment system serves over 15 million Americans a year, providing employment assistance, labor market, and other workforce-related information and services, and access to training through its One-Stop Delivery system. The workforce investment system, with its declining federal funding and structural limitations, is not adequate as a stand-alone program, to meet the overwhelming human capital needs of the United States today and in the future. State and

---

[18] Martin and Halperin, *Whatever It Takes.*

local workforce systems must act strategically to establish partnerships and leverage resources that will enable them to meet the increasingly complex employment and skill needs of job seekers, employers, and their regional economies in the future.[19]

At a time when federal budget deficits loom large in the United States, and domestic spending is sharply reduced, needless duplication and waste are not feasible. However, funding reductions seem to perversely result in the walling off of funding "silos" to protect dwindling budgets. As a result, partnering has become more difficult for states, and particularly for local workforce areas in the absence of specific federal requirement for system integration and resource sharing, and a lack of financial incentives for partnering.[20]

WIA took what was previously a targeted collection of programs (focused primarily on economically disadvantaged and dislocated workers) and established an employment and training system for all job seekers and for employers. The shift from 40 years of supply-side federal workforce policy that concentrated primarily on the job seeker to one that has employers as a primary customer has taken time. By loosening eligibility requirements, Congress intended that the WIA system would become more relevant for high-skill, high-wage employers, as well as more easily aligned with economic development efforts. However, a serious concern has emerged, in part as the result of the opening up of the One-Stops and their core services to a universal population. This expansion of responsibilities has resulted in an apparent reduction in WIA-funded training in many states and local areas, and in some areas a reduction in services for individuals with multiple barriers to employment.[21]

---

[19] Clagett, "Workforce Development in the United States."

[20] Ibid.

[21] Ibid.

V. RECOMMENDATIONS FOR POLICY AND FUNDING

Both the Adult Education and Family Literacy Act (Title II of WIA) and the WIA itself have been subject to reauthorization attempts since 2003. The major stumbling block for the 108th and 109th Congresses was the proposed insertion to the House Bill to allow faith-based training providers to discriminate on the basis of religion in the hiring of staff. These providers could not discriminate on the basis of those seeking training, only on the basis of employees working for the provider.

The 110th Congress has indicated that the AEFLA and WIA reauthorization is a top priority, and early action is expected. The faith-based provision will not likely be part of the final package, now that the Democrats are in the majority. Yet significant questions remain as to how Congress will reform the WIA. Will they collapse the separate funding streams for young people, adults, and dislocated workers? Will they eliminate the requirement for sequential tiers of core services, intensive services, and training services? Will they increase the minimum expenditure threshold for out-of-school youth? We should know the answers to these questions soon.

The National Center on Education and the Economy has **three recommendations** regarding funding and administration of adult education and job training:

- It is time to change the organization of the adult education and public job training functions in our society to better align them with the forces and institutions of economic development. To do this a federal budget increase will be necessary. There are few investments this country can make that are likely to have a greater payoff in improved productivity and economic growth.
- Create a personal competitiveness account for each newborn child. Contributions would be made by the U.S. government through age 16, then individuals and employers would be encouraged (through tax benefits) to make contributions. The federal government would match individual contributions for low-income workers.

- Recommend creating regional competitive authorities that blend regional economic development with regional workforce development to make America competitive and align these regions with community college districts. This would have all three parties working toward the same goal for the same region.[22]

According to John Wallace, the 2006 TANF reauthorization was, in part, a missed opportunity because the size of the welfare caseload in our country is at its lowest level since the early 1960s—meaning that the system could literally afford to take on the bigger issues. The TANF reauthorization experience may offer an important lesson for WIA reauthorization. There is an opportunity for the new Congress to take up some of the larger issues confronting the labor force now and in the coming years and to lay out an expanded vision for the workforce system that is also mindful of budget limits. Wallace made **six recommendations**:

- Expanding the target population: The substantially lower unemployment rate over the past 10 years and the increasing size of the low-wage workforce suggest that the workforce system must begin to tackle job advancement and retention issues.
- Working with employers on job retention and advancement and retraining: Employers in some sectors have advancement opportunities with their firms, and they see their incumbent low-wage workers as being strong potential candidates. MDRC is conducting, with support from the U.S. Department of Labor and several foundations, the Work Advancement and Support Center Demonstration in One-Stops in four cities.
- Very few One-Stops have housed work support eligibility staff from the welfare agency on site, and few One-Stops offer access to work supports for working people. Yet One-Stops are extremely well positioned—far better than welfare agencies—to provide an access point to work supports for

[22] NCEE, *Tough Choices or Tough Times.*

working people. Doing this would, of course, require developing close collaborative relationships with welfare agencies, which may not be the norm.

- A new set of performance standards would need to be developed that are appropriate to new populations. Performance standards should not drive the system to enroll people who would do as well, or nearly as well, on their own.
- With budget constraints in mind, this expanded vision might be undertaken through national grants in a number of select Workforce Investment Boards across the country so that their experiences and the lessons that grow out of their work can inform the next WIA reauthorization debate.
- The biggest issue has been a culture change. It requires a recognition that One-Stops would be working with *working* people, not just unemployed people. Working people by definitions have limited time availability and cannot be expected to wait for extensive application procedures or repeated call-backs to an office. It means that staff members often need to do their jobs at employer sites or other venues outside the One-Stop offices, rather that requiring customers to come in. And offices need to be open longer hours and on weekends, as they are in more of the rest of the service industry.[23]

Recommendation: Perhaps Commerce, Labor, and Education need more collaboration to solve a critical problem in the United States—our economic competitiveness is becoming less competitive. This would include jointly funded demonstrations and staffs working together to make sure benefits are not being duplicated, but also that there are no gaps in needed services.

VI. CONCLUSION

This chapter describes major federal funded programs that provide services to assist adults in increasing academic, life, and

[23] Wallace, *A Vision for the Future of the Workforce Investment System.*

jobs skills to successfully climb the career ladder. The goals are to help individuals and families become self-sufficient, productive members of U.S. society, to assist companies in obtaining the skilled workforce needed for positive productivity, and to keep this country economically competitive in an increasingly global marketplace.

The services provided to qualifying individuals are varied and many contribute only a small piece to the complete puzzle of what is needed to move people through the ACP pipeline to success. Some services provide education that supplies academic and technical knowledge to progress on the job, but several provide support services to help take care of basic needs such as healthcare, food, and childcare. Some of the services are focused on those at the younger end of the spectrum—"out-of-school youth"—who need to learn life skills such as self-discipline, communications, teamwork, and personal hygiene. Taking care of basic needs and life skills must take place before the individual can concentrate on what is needed to advance up the ladder.

In addition to describing services, the chapter reports the views of several organizations and individuals who have studied the nation's workforce development programs. These views include listing perceived problems as well as recommendations for improving the system. The greatest problems deal with the complexity of programs, the lack of collaboration that create gaps in services, and decreasing funding. The recommendations fall along the lines of fixing these perceived weaknesses in the patchwork of programs (more funding, more collaboration, and maximizing access to users). Particularly noteworthy among the "more funding" recommendations is the often-repeated suggestion of funding demonstration activities in a few selected locations, collecting good data, then expanding funding to replicate what works.

Federal programs do not exist in isolation from state and local funds and agencies, especially since most of the federal programs require some level of matching efforts from the providers of the services—but that is a topic for the next chapter.

Appendix

Federal Funding for Major (and other selected) Programs Dealing with Adult Career Pathways

Federal Funding Agency	Program Name	Funding Level in FY06	Purpose or Strategy	Target Population
Department of Labor (DOL)	Workforce Investment Act: 1. Youth Program 2. Adult Employment and Training 3. Dislocated Worker	1. $940 Million 2. $857 Million 3. $1.58 Billion	1. Assist high risk youth in completing education and training 2. Education and training through One-Stop centers. 3. Assistance for those terminated or laid off	1. Ages 14 to 21 2. Adults 3. Adult Dislocated Workers
DOL	Job Corps	$1.564 Billion	Residential academic, vocational, and social skills training	Disadvantaged youth ages 16 to 24
Department of Education (ED)	Carl D. Perkins Career and Technical Education Act	$1.296 Billion	To improve academic and career skills of students	High school and college youth and adults enrolled in career and technical courses
ED	Adult Education and Family Literacy Act	$579 Million	Fundamental literacy, ESL training, and GED test preparation	Adults and out-of-school youth ages 16 and older

Federal Funding Agency	Program Name	Funding Level in FY06	Purpose or Strategy	Target Population
ED	Pell Grants	$17.6 Billion	To assist students with paying college costs including tuition, books, room and board	College students demonstrating financial need
Department of Health and Human Services (HHS)	Temporary Assistance for Needy Families (TANF)	$17 Billion	Financial assistance for education, welfare-to-work, child care, and other social services	Low-income families with children
Department of Housing and Urban Development (HUD)	YouthBuild	$49.5 Million	Youth learn construction skills to rehabilitate housing while learning other developmental skills	High risk youth ages 16 to 24
Corporation for National and Community Service (CNCS) (an independent federal agency)	AmeriCorps	$290 Million	Trains volunteers for service to public agencies, nonprofits, and faith-based orgs. Members receive an education award which can pay for college or other training.	Ages 17 and older
Department of Defense (DOD)	Montgomery GI Bill	$192 Million	Educational benefits for military veterans	Honorably discharged veterans with high school diploma or GED

Chapter 11 Preview

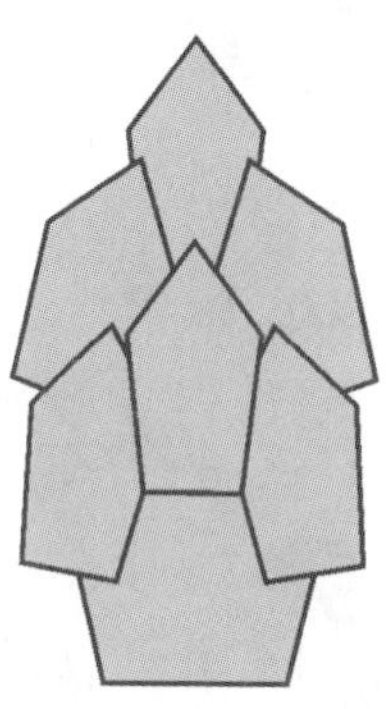

Like federal workforce development programs, state programs focus primarily on short-term training and entry-level skills. Full-fledged ACP programs would reshape that vision into "second-chance" education that enables adults not only to reenter the workforce in rewarding career pathways, but to gain the academic foundations and employability skills necessary to continue their education and job growth along well-defined career ladders. The ACP model is "front-loaded" with a full-time Prep Stage (one semester of college courses), during which the average ACP student will require significant amounts of financial and "in-kind" support (transportation, housing, childcare, and so on). In the subsequent stages (2–10), the student and participating employer assume more of the costs as federal and state costs diminish. (See Chapter 9, "Who Foots the Bill?") This chapter identifies state policies and funding sources that could be accessed to help ACP students, particularly during the Prep Stage. Many of the identified state programs are actually federal programs that are managed at the state level. Every state should also be able to come up with some level of state funding. State leaders and lawmakers are encouraged to consider coherent policies that address the ACP vision. As this chapter points out, our future depends on it.

DH & RH

STATE POLICY MODELS TO SUPPORT ADULT CAREER PATHWAYS

Kathy D'Antoni and Debra Mills

INTRODUCTION

The current economic climate does not bode well for low-skill adults. Industrial jobs are being lost to foreign workers at an alarming pace, and more and more of the remaining jobs demand some level of postsecondary education. As public revenue streams shrink and state and local budgets are cut, it is becoming increasingly difficult for struggling adults—the people targeted in the ACP vision presented in this book—to get help in acquiring the higher-level skills they urgently need.

One of the main reasons so many American corporations are moving their operations overseas is that they can't find enough high-skilled workers here. As the focus of our economy shifts from manufacturing to knowledge-based fields such as information technology, the gap between what American employers need and what they can actually find will continue to widen. The problem is nationwide. Every state in America faces a workforce crisis.

More and more governors are coming to the realization that the economic health of their states will ultimately be determined not by their natural resources but by the skills of their citizens—their "human capital." The availability of highly qualified workers is the single most decisive factor in determining whether states can attract and keep strong, growing businesses. To preserve their human capital, states must be willing to make, monitor, and sustain significant investments in the skills of their citizens. That is the topic of this chapter.

One of the main strengths of the ACP concept is that its implementation would create situations in which everyone wins. ACP student-employees improve the quality of their lives, employer partners gain high-quality workers, and communities are relieved of burdens associated with care for the poor, to name only a few of the benefits. States would win as well. While the ACP concept calls for significant investment at the state level, it would yield a very high return. Specifically, ACP programs would benefit states in at least six ways:

1. By providing a pipeline of employees who are able to meet the workforce needs of employers
2. By improving the earning power and self-sufficiency of low-income workers
3. By creating an environment in which educators, businesspeople, and public officials are *jointly* involved in the formulation of state workforce and economic development policy
4. By leading to a more efficient and effective use of publicly allocated workforce development and education resources
5. By creating a mechanism for holding workforce development systems accountable for results
6. By providing a system that enables current and dislocated workers to retrain and retool

ALIGNING STATE VISION WITH ACP

Every state devotes resources to workforce training. But most of the workforce development policies currently in place tend to stress quick-fix, work-first training programs and do little to help struggling adults acquire the foundational academic and technical skills necessary to raise their standards of living over time. Several published reports indicate that people placed in entry-level jobs after short-term job training still earn well below the poverty level and are no more financially stable than they were prior to training.

If states were to align their visions for workforce development activities with the ACP concept, the narrow, short-term focus of most current workforce development activities would give way to more lasting, comprehensive approaches that change people's lives and give employers the confidence to establish deep roots in their communities. Widespread implementation of ACP would also engage the private sector and the entire spectrum of public-to-private education and training, thereby creating a dynamic synergy that would promote every state's economic growth and stability.[1]

Our research on states' workforce development models has led us to conclude that few states, if any, have put in place policies that fully capture the intent of the ACP concept. Several state models include *components* of ACP, but no state has implemented the ACP concept in its entirety.[2]

The creation of ACP programs calls for state-level policies that support at least three things: *accessibility, affordability,* and *sustainability*. As states examine how their policies might be

---

[1] Martin Simon and Linda Hoffman, *The Next Generation of Workforce Development Project: A Six-State Policy Academy to Enhance Connections Between Workforce and Economic Development Policy* (report to U.S. Department of Labor, Employment and Training Administration, 2004).

[2] Julian L. Alssid, David Gruber, Davis Jenkins, Christopher Mazzeo, Brandon Roberts, and Regina Stanback-Stroud, *Building a Career Pathways System: Promising Practices in Community College-Centered Workforce Development* (Workforce Strategy Center, 2002).

changed to support ACP programs, they should do everything possible to ensure that those programs are accessible and affordable to every state resident who needs them, and can be sustained over time. The following remarks examine each of those areas in more detail and provide recommendations on how states can address them.

Accessibility

One of the ironies of "second chance" education programs is that they are much better known among people who don't need them than among people who do. Most economically and educationally disadvantaged adults are largely unaware of the services available to them and do not know how to put together assistance packages that will improve their quality of life. For them, in effect, access to the programs has been denied.

State Policy Actions to Ensure Accessibility

To ensure program accessibility, every state should establish policies that accomplish the following:

1. Set forth a state-specific vision for workforce education in which the private sector plays a key role.
   - The vision would include policies that engage the private sector and the entire spectrum of education and training (both public and private). Existing workforce policies that promote narrow job training must give way to policies that meet long-term needs of the state's employers as a whole, along with needs of its current and emerging workforce.
2. Create a state-level partnership in which businesspeople, educators, and policymakers *jointly* develop a comprehensive framework for ACP.
   - In most states, workforce development is offered piecemeal: Multiple agencies deliver education and training in isolation from one another, complex administrative requirements differ from one agency to the next, and there is no statewide system of

accountability. The ACP concept demands that state agencies in education and workforce and economic development align their efforts and collaborate in setting policies that pertain to adult education.

3. Develop clear, easy-to-understand pathways that enable career-limited adults to progress step-by-step through programs that lead to postsecondary credentials in high-demand fields.
   - Over the last few years, the responsibility for career advancement has shifted from companies to individuals. Providers of career education and supporting information have been slow to respond to that change. As a result, many adults who recognize the need to improve their career skills don't know how to go about it, and don't know how to get the necessary financial assistance. Well-supported, clearly defined state-level ACP programs would remedy that problem.
4. Encourage the development of "bridge" programs designed to teach a combination of basic literacy and numeracy, work-readiness skills, and career-specific skills.
   - Career-limited adults often need a little extra help before they can even begin ACP programs. Bridge programs are designed to help adults close their skill gaps so that they can move forward toward self-sufficiency and career advancement.

Affordability

Much of the cost of individual ACP programs must be borne by entities other than the ACP students themselves, especially during the earliest stages. This is a fundamental aspect of the ACP concept. If career-limited adults are to take advantage of ACP opportunities in large numbers, the programs must be affordable to *anyone*. This means that, for states (among other entities), implementation of ACP programs will carry a high price tag. However—and this too is fundamental to the ACP concept—the rewards garnered by states will far outweigh the costs.

Making ACP programs universally affordable will require that states use their resources as efficiently as possible. States should first take stock of the resources they are spending on adult education and workforce training. Using those findings, states will be able to (1) determine how resources from separate programs might be combined, (2) identify gaps in funding, and (3) identify areas in which partnering with private enterprises and community-based organizations would produce additional resources.

State Policy Actions to Ensure Affordability

To ensure program affordability, every state should establish policies that accomplish the following:

1. Provide financial aid programs specifically for adults entering ACP programs
   - Adults who want to go back to school are caught between two opposing forces. One is that fewer and fewer employers are willing to pay for workforce training. The other is that postsecondary education is becoming more expensive all the time. For many adults, especially those who stand to gain most from ACP programs, the expense of postsecondary education—even at low-cost community and technical colleges—is prohibitive. Outside of WIA dollars, few, if any, financial aid programs specifically target low-wage, low-skilled adults. States should establish funds to provide financial aid specifically for adults in ACP programs and "bridge" programs that prepare adults to enter ACP programs.
2. Blend resources from existing state and federal funding streams such as WIA, TANF, Carl D. Perkins, and Adult Basic Education, for the purpose of supporting a state-level ACP strategy.
   - The fragmentation of most states' workforce development activities causes confusion and

duplication of effort. Adult Basic Education, Carl D. Perkins, Welfare to Work, WIA, and other public programs have similar goals—to improve the American workforce. However, the entities that administer those programs rarely, if ever, collaborate. The result is duplication of effort and waste of state revenues.

3. Increase financial support for postsecondary education institutions that provide ACP courses and supporting services.
   - Implementation of ACP programs will create additional expense for the postsecondary education institutions (specifically community and technical colleges) that will provide ACP courses and supporting services such as curriculum and standards development, "bridge programs," training programs for employer mentors, and professional development for volunteer teachers associated with community and faith-based organizations. A state-level funding stream earmarked specifically for ACP would give postsecondary education institutions both the incentive and the means to participate in ACP programs.
4. Provide higher FTE funding for postsecondary career preparation programs that specifically serve low-income, low-skill adults.
   - Because they are typically low-skill and low-wage (or no-wage, if unemployed), ACP students need extra help, especially in the early stages of their programs. To help meet the cost of the additional support services required, states should give postsecondary institutions higher FTE funding for people enrolled in ACP programs.

Sustainability

Many government programs are only as long-lasting as the funding programs that support them. When funding runs out, the programs stop. What we envision for ACP is more durable. With the right state policies in place, ACP programs can withstand the ups and downs of economic fluctuations, changes in state and federal administrations, and other trends that might adversely affect workforce development programs. To be successful, ACP programs must be sustainable. The entities that are asked to invest in those programs, especially businesses, must have a reasonable assurance that the programs will be around for a long time.

State Policy Actions to Ensure Sustainability

To ensure program sustainability, every state should establish policies that accomplish the following:

1. Support the development of ACP program performance standards that ensure accountability and reward success.
   - The process of creating and sustaining ACP programs should be governed by clear expectations as to what the participating entities—employers, educators, policymakers, community and faith-based organizations—should do, and how they will know whether they are doing it right. Without clearly defined performance standards, ACP programs will lack consistency; some partners will become discouraged and drop out. This recommendation includes the understanding that programs would provide annual reports to their state legislatures on progress and challenges.
2. Use Adult Basic Education (ABE) dollars to develop basic skills that meet ACP entrance requirements.
   - People who lack basic literacy and numeracy skills will not be able to succeed in ACP programs. To increase the number of people who are ACP-ready, ABE programs should teach skills that are specifically tailored to ACP entrance requirements. In turn, ACP programs should try to match their entrance requirements with the skills that can be taught in ABE programs. To the extent possible, ABE program goals

and ACP entrance requirements should align. Whether this becomes a reality should not be left to the discretion of individual programs. It should be established at the state level.

3. Strengthen the governance and accountability of the state's workforce development system.
   - Carrying out this recommendation would involve the creation of systemwide performance indicators that gage the extent to which each branch of the system contributes to the state's overall economic health.
4. Connect workforce development programs to the needs of employers.
   - The ACP concept is based on the belief that employers should be able to find well-trained workers locally, and that workers should be able to find good jobs in the communities where they live. For those things to happen, ACP programs must be tailored to the needs of employers—current and future—at both local and state levels. States should conduct whatever research is necessary to be sure they know the real needs of their employers and how those needs are likely to change in the foreseeable future. Every state's workforce development policies should be closely integrated with its economic development policies so that businesses in the state can find good employees and the state's citizens can achieve lifelong success in careers.

PROMISING PRACTICES IN WEST VIRGINIA AND ILLINOIS

At the outset of this chapter, we said that, while many states have in place successful components of ACP, no state has implemented the ACP concept in its entirety. The following pages describe promising ACP models in West Virginia and Illinois. The reason for examining these two models in detail is this: One of the key points we hope to convey in this book is that implementation of ACP would not amount to reinventing the wheel. The entities involved would not be asked to do something radically different from what they are already doing. In many states, getting from the status quo to fully functional ACP programs would involve mainly a new level of coordination and collaboration, especially between the public and private sectors.

Toward the beginning of this chapter, we said that the success of ACP programs will ultimately depend on states' ability to ensure that the programs have three basic qualities: *accessibility, affordability,* and *sustainability.* As we examine the models in West Virginia and Illinois, we will focus specifically on how they demonstrate those qualities.

West Virginia

Accessibility

By executive order, the Governor of West Virginia created a state-level Workforce Planning Council consisting of representatives of postsecondary education, workforce development, economic development, public education, and the governor's cabinet. Their mission is to work together as a unit to coordinate initiatives, leverage resources, and plan for the delivery of a comprehensive workforce strategy that meets the educational and training needs of the state's employers and citizens in four targeted industries (Figure 11-1). The resulting model, which is designed to ensure program access for *all* state residents, is an excellent example of how multiple state-level entities can join forces in developing and delivering career pathways through state-financed training programs in targeted industries.

To ensure accessibility, the West Virginia model is designed to meet the needs of three groups of people, who, taken collectively, constitute the entire spectrum of people who stand to benefit from ACP programs:

1. People with few skills and little or no workplace experience
2. People currently employed in minimum wage jobs
3. People who seek to upgrade their skills

Affordability

In 2004, West Virginia enacted legislation that created the Higher Education Adult Part-Time Scholarships (HEAPS) program. HEAPS is a unique state-funded financial aid package designed to encourage and enable needy West Virginians to continue their education through workforce training academies and other programs that lead to industry-recognized credentials. In addition, the HEAPS program helps the state meet its economic development goals by granting funds to community and technical colleges that develop and deliver workforce training programs.

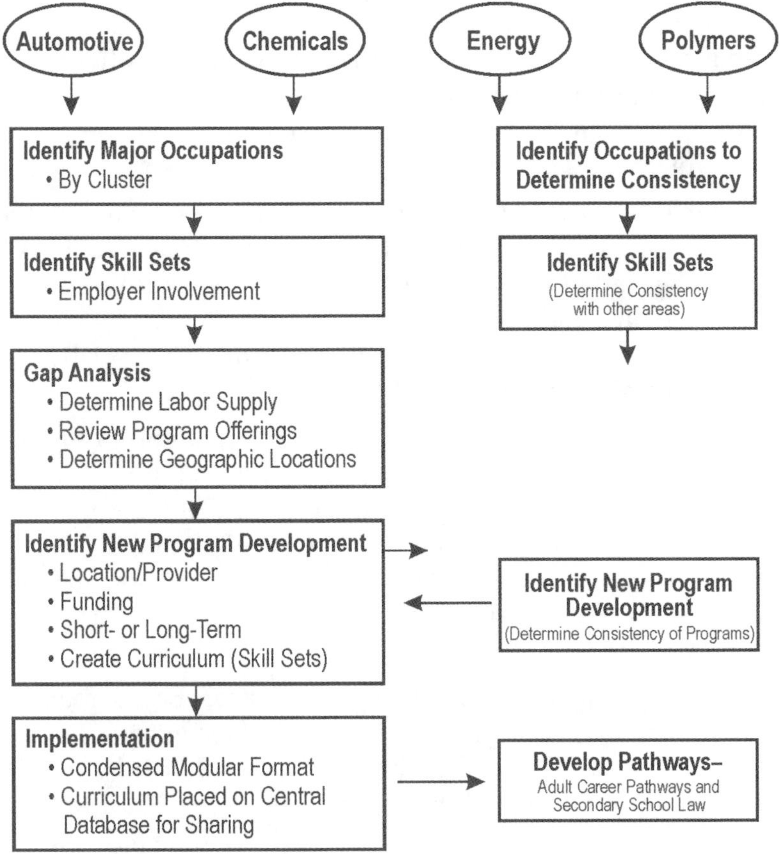

Figure 11-1. Development Process for Career Pathways in West Virginia

Sustainability

In 2004, West Virginia began to investigate an ACP model. The state was looking for a way to build a strong workforce by connecting education, economic development, and workforce development. West Virginia believed that this collaboration would give current and displaced workers the opportunity to upgrade their skills and would establish a pipeline of qualified workers. As a result of the partnership, an ACP prototype was created (Figure 11-2). The ACP concept has still not been fully implemented, but a number of the components have been legislated.

The West Virginia ACP system is sustainable because it is mandated at the state level and enjoys the commitment of a broad range of partners—community and technical colleges, community-based organizations, adult basic education, workforce investment boards, and employers. Each plays a unique role, as described below:

- *The role of community and technical colleges*—As the hub of the ACP system as a whole, community and technical colleges take the lead in pathway development. They cultivate partnerships and provide synergy and expertise. They also serve as the gateway to continuing education, especially for economically disadvantaged persons.
- *The role of community-based organizations*—Community-based organizations augment the colleges' limited resources by identifying, recruiting, and providing supplementary services to potential participants who are isolated from postsecondary education institutions. These organizations provide invaluable support services to participants as they progress through the ACP system.
- *The role of Adult Basic Education*—Adult Basic Education acts as an equal partner with community and technical colleges in providing preparatory education. They work hand in hand with community and technical colleges to develop and provide "bridge" programs that help struggling adults gain the reading and math skills necessary for admission to community and technical college programs.

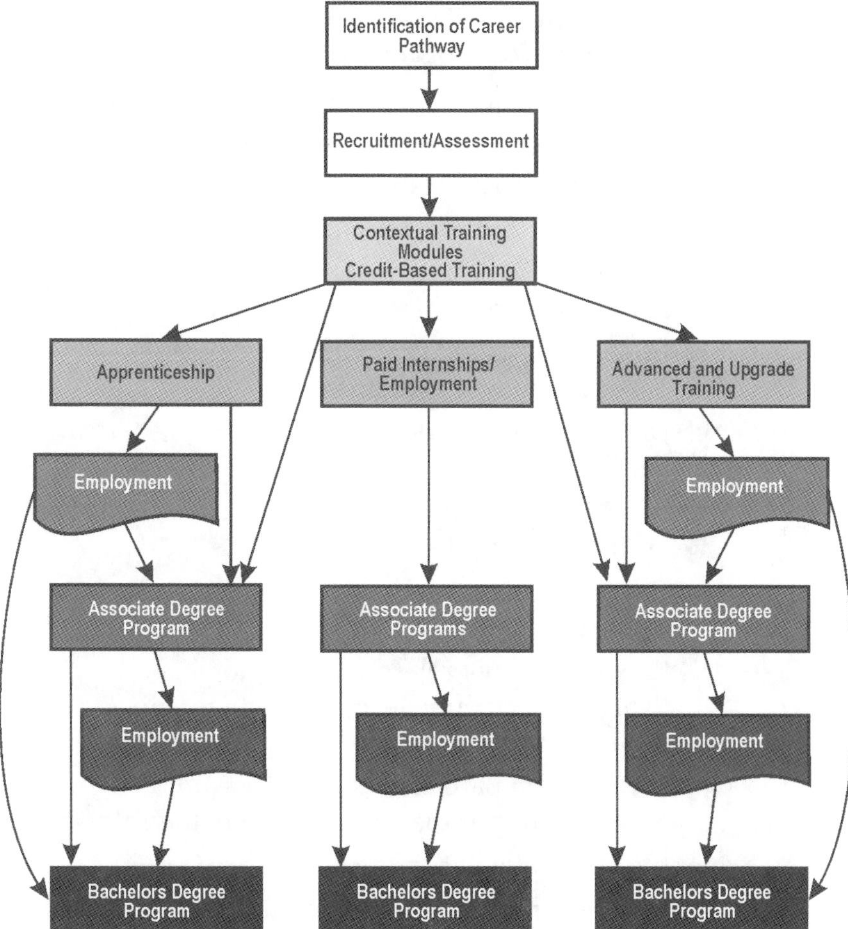

Figure 11-2. The West Virginia Career Pathways Model

- *The role of local workforce investment boards*—Local workforce investment boards (WIB) identify cluster needs in their regions and facilitate development of training programs to be delivered by the community and technical colleges that serve those regions. WIBs also support the ACP system through student recruitment and financial aid. All efforts are designed to increase the return on the workforce development investment.
- *The role of local employers*—Local employers help training providers to know precisely what knowledge and skills they

require of their employees. They also provide internships and other worksite learning opportunities.

In the West Virginia model, ACP partners carry out the following steps in developing each pathway program:

1. Develop an overview of the pathway.
2. Determine the main components of the pathway.
   a. Identify ACP milestones (entry and exit points) (Job placement is considered an exit point.)
   b. Community-based organizations and WIBs recruit potential student participants
   c. Deliver pathway orientation to potential student participants
   d. Assess the skill and academic proficiency levels and needs of potential students
   e. Develop contextual instructional modules based on assessment results
   f. Provide faculty professional development designed to help participating faculty members gain proficiency in teaching to multiple learning styles
   g. Give student participants the opportunity to earn college credits as they move through the pathway
3. Identify areas in which partners can share resources
4. Assess program outcomes on a regular basis (at least annually)

This model has served as a starting point for the West Virginia ACP system. To date, one pathway has been developed and is being implemented: The Nursing Adult Career Pathway Program.

Illinois

Illinois is one of the top states in the percentage of working-age adults (ages 25 to 49) enrolled part-time in college-level education or training.[3] This fact indicates that, on the whole, state residents have high individual expectations for education and that the state provides enough spaces and types of educational programs for its residents. It also suggests that the Illinois system is *accessible, affordable,* and *sustainable,* to return to our three focus areas. The following remarks describe how Illinois maintains those qualities in its adult education programs.

Accessibility

Illinois' community colleges are the state's major skills-development and career preparation institutions, particularly for low-income workers. Among postsecondary institutions in Illinois, community colleges enroll by far the highest proportion of low-income residents (particularly from inner-city areas), foreign-born residents, and minorities. Fifty-eight percent (211,676 students) are women.[4] In part because of its broad accessibility, the Illinois Community College System is the foundation of the state's efforts to help greater numbers of adults work their way through career preparation programs and succeed in rewarding careers.

Affordability

Illinois has one of the most generous financial aid systems in the country, providing nearly $500 million to college students each year. Nonetheless, that amount still falls far short of the amount that would be needed to support fully functional ACP programs statewide. In the current system, students are burdened with an increasingly heavy share of the college cost. For the state's poorest families, the cost of attending a community college, *even after aid,* is over one-third of the annual household income, and

---

[3] "Measuring Up 2006–Illinois Report" The National Center For Public Policy and Higher Education http://measuringup.highereducation.org

[4] Illinois Community College Board, "Facts About Community Colleges" (ICCB website) and Illinois Community College Board, "Data and Characteristics of the Illinois Public Community College System, 2005."

ratio of cost to household income rises to more than one-half for public four-year universities. The Silas Purnell Illinois Incentive for Access (IIA) provides assistance to the lowest-income students, but the program is limited to nontuition expenses such as books and transportation and pays only $1000 per student (womenemployed.org).

In addition to the IIA, Illinois has created the Monetary Award Program (MAP), a need-based financial assistance program for low-income college students. The MAP provides grants to Illinois residents who demonstrate financial need. However, the MAP has been underfunded in the last several years and has lost its purchasing power.[5]

Grants are critically important to low-income students. For them, the high *relative* cost of nontuition items such as books and transportation can place postsecondary education and training out of reach. According to a 2003 report from the U.S. Department of Transportation, people with annual incomes of less than $8,000 spent nearly 10 percent of their incomes commuting in 1999, while those with incomes of $45,000 or more spent just 2 percent.[6]

Illinois is a national leader in providing state-funded financial incentives for low-income students. But implementation of the ACP concept will call for a reexamination of the state's funding formula, especially for residents with the greatest financial needs.

Sustainability

Over the past four years, Illinois has taken a new approach to workforce development, bringing together regional and local workforce development, economic development, and education partners through a strategy based on industry sectors. The Illinois Community College Board and the Illinois Department

---

[5] *Mapping a Future for Illinois' Economy and Families: A Plan to Invest in Financial Aid for Low-Income Students* (Women Employed Institute, 2003).

[6] Jeffrey Ball, "Fueling Frustration for Many Low-Income Workers, High Gasoline Prices Take a Toll," *The Wall Street Journal,* 12 July 2004.

of Commerce and Economic Opportunity (DCEO, the workforce and economic development arm of the state) have partnered in the following ways to address the state's workforce needs through "bridge" and career pathway initiatives:

1. Early on, Illinois community college presidents pledged to support development of ten Economic Development Regions (EDR).
2. The EDRs were created to allow for regionalization of workforce and economic development initiatives and to allow for a more efficient use of funding. Although community colleges and adult education providers were already collaborating with the workforce and economic development entities in the newly defined regions, creation the EDRs enhanced existing partnerships and gave their work a sharper focus on regional needs.
3. CSSI/Industry Sector Strategies—The first major initiative to be implemented as a result of the EDRs was the Critical Skill Shortages Initiative, the purpose of which was to allow the regions to develop and implement industry sector initiatives that were specific to them. DCEO funded those initiatives, with the regional industry sector needs being determined by regional partners including employers, community colleges, other educational partners, workforce and economic development entities, and others. The industry sectors to be identified by the EDRs were healthcare, transportation distribution and logistics (TDL), and manufacturing. Funds flow through the local workforce investment boards (LWIB), with many community colleges as subrecipients of funding for training, capacity building, and retention efforts.
4. The Illinois Community College Board decided to align workforce efforts with the CSSI/industry sector approach being implemented by DCEO. ICCB chose to use its portion of the WIA Incentive funds and other WIA funds each year to align with the industry sectors being rolled out—healthcare, TDL, and manufacturing. Because the ICCB administers the Adult Education and Family

Literacy Act and the postsecondary Perkins, adult education and Perkins have been involved in the development and implementation of the pilots. Over the last three years the Illinois Community College Board has provided over $4 million in grant opportunities through an RFP process to many of the community colleges to pilot-test bridge program initiatives in healthcare and TDL. Manufacturing will be the next bridge pilot. Additionally, ICCB is funding healthcare bridge pilots addressing blended on-line learning and the use of technology with low-skilled, low-income persons. Many lessons are being learned from the pilot bridge programs (some of which are highlighted through work done by Women Employed; see below). As a result of the many efforts taking place around bridge programs and transition services, the Illinois Council of Public Community College Presidents created a Bridge Task Force to examine bridge programs and to develop funding recommendations. Additionally, a Joint Task Force on Community Colleges charged by the Illinois state legislature to conduct a review of the Illinois Community College System, recommended bridge /transition programs through two of its subcommittees.[7]

Bridge Programs in Illinois

In 2003, Women Employed (an advocacy group) launched the Illinois Career Pathways Initiative, a collaborative effort designed to enable individuals of varied skill and ability levels to progress along clearly defined educational pathways and into good jobs. This advocacy group has been joined by the Chicago Jobs Council, whose mission is to ensure access to employment and career-advancement opportunities for people in poverty in the Chicago area, and by the Great Cities Institute (GCI), which serves as the University of Illinois at Chicago's (UIC) focal point

---

[7] Lavon Nelson, Director for Workforce Systems, Illinois Community College Board (personal communication, February 26, 2007).

for new initiatives in interdisciplinary applied urban research.[8] Joined by the Workforce Boards of Metropolitan Chicago, this partnership has focused on the development of the first rung of the pathway—*bridge programs* for low-literate individuals who are locked in low-wage jobs or are unemployed.[9] The programs serve adults at two levels, lower and higher.

- *Lower-level bridge programs*—Adults who are unemployed or in lower-level semiskilled jobs are placed in lower-level bridge programs. Later these adults can advance to higher-level semiskilled jobs and to higher levels of training, including more advanced bridge programs. The lower-level programs are generally designed for native English speakers at the fifth- or sixth-grade reading level or for non-native speakers at the low-to-intermediate ESL level. Although participants in the programs are usually far from qualifying for college-level training or career-path employment, they begin to explore postsecondary and career opportunities as part of the bridge experience.[10]
- *Higher-level bridge programs*—If a student is reading at the seventh-grade level (native speaker) or an intermediate-to-high level for ESL, the student can enter the higher-level bridge program. This level prepares adults for advancement into entry-level skilled positions and into occupational certificate or associate degree programs. These programs are focused on occupation-specific skills, which include basic skills (reading, communication, and applied math) integrated with teaching of basic occupation-specific technical skills. They are usually offered at colleges but can also be offered at workplaces. Workplace delivery usually happens when state customized training and workplace

---

[8] www.womenemployed.org/docs/Career%20Pathways%20Initiative.pdf

[9] *Bridges to Careers for Low-Skilled Adults: A Program Development Guide* (2005), http://www.womenemployed.org/index.php?id=27.

[10] *Bridges to Careers for Low-Skilled Adults: A Program Development Guide* (2005).

literacy funds are linked to develop programs for advancing employees within individual companies or employer consortia (Figure 11-3).

Target Audience	• Seventh-to-eighth-grade reading (for native English speakers) • High-intermediate ESL level (for non-native speakers) • With or without a high school diploma or GED • Stable work history • Desire to pursue postsecondary technical training or education
Job Objective—Full-time job paying $8 to $12 per hour, usually with benefits. Examples include bank teller, multiple machine tool setter, medical billing, and coding clerk.	**Education Objective**—College-level certificate, associate degree program, or other postsecondary technical training
Duration	8–16 weeks, 12–14 hours per week
Features	• Outcome competencies set by employers and college occupational degree program faculty • Basic reading (reading for information), writing (paragraphs), speaking (presentations), math (prealgebra), and computer applications (word processing, spreadsheet, presentation software) taught in the context of exploring careers and postsecondary training options and preparing a career plan • Learning success skills (for school and on the job), including note-taking, study habits, time management, financial literacy, and test-taking • Training in industry-specific vocabulary and technical fundamentals taught using workplace problems and tools and material from introductory college-level courses (in field-specific programs) • College credits or "credit equivalencies" for competencies developed and documented during bridge training • Job shadowing and internships • Job and college placement assistance
Program Examples	• Watsonville Digital Bridge Academic, Cabrillo College • WAGE Pathways Bridge Program, Southeast Arkansas • College and Southern Good Faith Fund • Manufacturing Technology Bridge, Instituto del Progreso Latino • Essential Skills Program, Community College of Denver

Figure 11-3. Higher-Level Bridge Program Model
(Source: *Bridges to Careers for Low-Skilled Adults: A Program Development Guide,* 2005)

Women Employed and the Chicago Jobs Council found that far too many Illinois families are not making ends meet, despite full-time employment. In a paper titled *In Making the Pieces Fit: A Plan for Ensuring a Prosperous Illinois*, the partnership examined Illinois' economic and workforce development systems, work supports programs, and workplace practices and offered recommendations for what can be done to ensure prosperity for all Illinois families:[11]

- *Integrate adult and vocational education*. Programs that teach basic literacy, numeracy, and language skills in a vocational skills training context produce greater educational and employment outcomes for the many adults who want to enter occupational training but cannot meet entrance requirements due to low basic skills.
- *Meet the demand for need-based financial aid*. Cuts in program funding have resulted in early suspension of awards, shrinking grant amounts, and elimination of grants for those who most urgently need higher education assistance. These disproportionately affect the state's most disadvantaged residents, those most in need of preparation to meet employer demand for a skilled workforce.
- *Improve performance accountability*. Illinois should track and regularly report on the earnings of students in all areas of the postsecondary education and training system, particularly low-income students.
- *Link education and training to economic development by supporting short-term noncredit coursework*. When possible, noncredit coursework should be linked to credit coursework as part of a career pathway approach. Illinois can better integrate its postsecondary education system with economic development goals by providing support to institutions and students for this type of training.

---

[11] www.womenemployed.org/docs/Making%20the%20Pieces%20Fit%20-%20Executive%20Summary.pdf.

- *Leverage Workforce Investment Act (WIA) and Temporary Assistance for Needy Families (TANF) dollars to build skills.* WIA and TANF funds should be used by local areas and the state to bridge individuals with limited skills into intensive vocational training for career path jobs and/or postsecondary education.

In Illinois (and elsewhere), bridge programs can serve an essential role in preparing adults for ACP programs. For most struggling adults, the pathway to better jobs leads through higher education. Bridge programs provide the initial steps in a longer progression that enables adults to advance over time to higher levels of education and rewarding employment.

Illinois is exploring ways to address the sustainability issues and other issues limiting the ability of the community colleges and adult education providers to deliver bridge programs. Although it is wonderful to be able to provide the pilot bridge initiatives, the real need is to be able to continue the initiatives and to expand opportunities to other community colleges. One way in which ICCB intends to continue the bridge pilots and, ultimately, answer some issues surrounding sustainability and access is through a recent grant from the Joyce Foundation. In 2006, ICCB, in partnership with DCEO and other entities such as Women Employed, applied for a Shifting Gears Initiative grant. The grant was awarded to ICCB in December 2006. The initiative will explore policy change through the use of demonstration projects in two key areas: (1) adult education to postsecondary credit programs and (2) remediation to community college credit.[12]

---

[12] Lavon Nelson, Director for Workforce Systems, Illinois Community College Board (personal communication, February 26, 2007).

CONCLUSION

Millions of American adults lack the skills necessary to enter and succeed in postsecondary education and advanced skills training—the keys to success in today's workplace. As the descriptions of West Virginia and Illinois in this chapter indicate, positive steps are already being taken. Like our federal government, every state in the union tries to help its struggling adults in some way. But those efforts tend to be disjointed and uncoordinated. Our overall approach to adult education must change in a fundamental way. We cannot afford to "throw away" our nation's economically and educationally disadvantaged adults. What is needed in states is not just welfare to work, but a system of pathways that enable student-employees to climb career ladders. This will require more collaboration between community colleges, employers, and workforce and economic development agencies.

The large and growing need for adult education translates into an equally large and growing burden on community colleges, our primary providers of remedial education. Something must be done to relieve that burden. Even in states such as West Virginia and Illinois, which are presented here as a promising foreshadowing of what *could* be, more funding is needed for educational and support services specifically targeted to the special needs of struggling adults.

If states expect their economies to be globally competitive, governors and legislators must start doing things differently. They must obtain commitments from key collaborators and provide state funding that can be coordinated with the federal funding that flows through their offices.

As a nation, we must find a way to get our struggling adults back into education and ultimately into the workplace, functioning at levels that are consistent with their natural abilities. States have a very important role to play in that process, and they must be willing to step forward and do their part. Our future depends on it.

APPENDIX: ILLINOIS STATE AND LOCAL FUNDS FOR BRIDGE PROGRAMS

State Funds

Adult Education and State General Revenue, like WIA Title II funds, are meant to assist those who lack basic educational skills (including reading, numeracy, and English language skills), do not have high school diploma or GEDs, or lack literacy in English. They are administered by the Illinois Community College Board.

Illinois' **Child Care for Education & Training** program serves families who are receiving Temporary Assistance for Needy Families (TANF) and participating in education and training in accordance with their responsibility and service plans and teen parents seeking high school diplomas or equivalent. In addition, the program serves families who work, do not receive TANF, and are pursuing additional education to improve their job opportunities. The program is administered by IDHS. Families can get childcare subsidies through the use of certificates or contracts.

Illinois' **Cooperative Work Study Program** provides grants to higher education institutions to support education-related work experiences that benefit students educationally and financially. Colleges submit proposals for funding to the Illinois Board of Higher Education and are expected to leverage employer matching funds if possible. Priority is given to supporting students who are Illinois residents.

Illinois **Full Time Equivalence** (FTE) grants are direct financial assistance to eligible postsecondary institutions based on the number of enrolled full-time-equivalent students. Colleges' use of FTE dollars must be outlined in their current operating budgets. Therefore, use of these funds for bridge programs would have to be indicated in the institution's next fiscal year budget.

Job Training and Economic Development (JTED) funds are designed to foster local economic development by addressing the needs of low-wage, low-skilled workers and disadvantaged individuals, as well as the workforce needs of local industry.

JTED Category I funding supports training of workers who earn $12.31/hour or less. JTED Category II supports training of unemployed, disadvantaged individuals. Community-based providers work in partnership with local businesses to provide training to persons enrolled in the program to meet the skill needs of local industry. Grants are competitively awarded through the Illinois Department of Commerce and Economic Opportunity (DCEO). Eligible providers are not-for-profit organizations with local boards of directors that directly provide job-training services.

The **Monetary Award Program** is Illinois' need-based tuition assistance grant for low-income students. Illinois students in credit-bearing programs are automatically considered for the MAP grant when they submit the Free Application for Federal Student Aid (FAFSA). Less-than-half-time students are eligible for this grant. The amount of the grant is determined by a formula that considers the student's ability to pay and the cost of attendance. The grant is administered by the Illinois Student Assistance Commission.

Silas Purnell Illinois Incentive for Access (IIA) program provides a one-time stipend to extremely low-income freshmen to offset the cost of nontuition expenses such as books and transportation. Illinois students in credit-bearing programs are automatically considered for the IIA stipend when they submit the Free Application for Federal Student Aid (FAFSA). The stipend is administered by the Illinois Student Assistance Commission.

The Illinois Secretary of State's **Workplace Skills Enhancement Grant Program** provides on-site instructional services to employees of Illinois businesses to enable them to enhance their basic reading, math, writing or language skills, maintain their employment, and increase their eligibility for promotion. Individual grants are awarded to businesses that match the award and operate in partnership with educational provider agencies.

Local Funds

Chicago's **TIFWorks** funds are meant to defray an employer's cost of developing or purchasing customized training programs tailored to his or her specific needs. Manufacturing companies and businesses must demonstrate that training will make them more competitive and directly benefit Chicago residents. Training providers must identify multiple businesses with common workforce development needs and must provide training and follow-up to their new hires and/or current employees. Companies must be located within, expanding into, or relocating to an eligible TIF district. Contracts are competitively awarded through the Chicago Mayor's Office of Workforce Development.[13]

---

[13] W. Smith and R. Unruh, *Building Bridges: Funding Options for the Core Components of Bridge programs*" (Women Employed: Illinois Career Pathways Initiative, Chicago, Illinois, May 2004).

Chapter 12 Preview

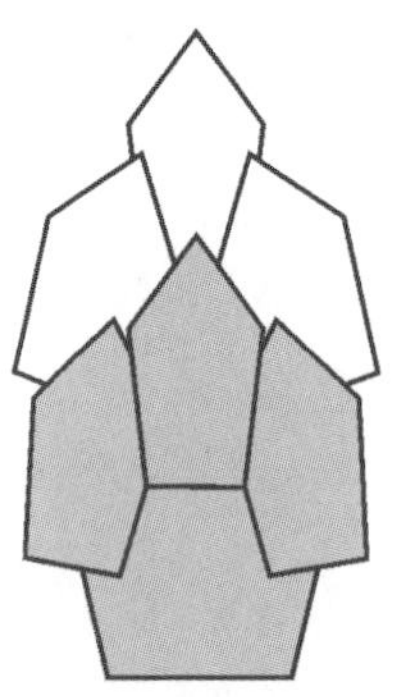

Throughout this book, we have shown how ACP programs attempt to solve both an economic development problem and a social problem. It's pretty easy to prove the value of ACP in light of the economic benefits of a world-class workforce for employers, states, and communities. But attaching a dollar figure to the social and human benefits of helping adults improve their lifestyles (particularly when many of them aren't very lovable) is much harder to pinpoint – and, in many cases, to "sell."

But Americans have a great heart and respect for the dignity of human life. We are blessed with community and national charities, generous philanthropists, and faith-based organizations where all citizens can volunteer their talents, time, and money in ways where they can see the fruits of their labor.

ACP programs are totally dependent on the 'in-kind" contributions that these organizations can organize and contribute.

The authors of this chapter tell us who these organizations are and where they are to be found. And they also remind us that all these organizations already have full agendas and ample, important demands on their resources. So, if we are to engage them in the ACP mission, we will have to seek them out, understand their missions, and find ways that their partnerships with ACP programs can be mutually supportive.

DH & RH

Community, Faith-Based, and Local Organizations to Support Adult Career Pathways

Pamela Gist and John Souders

Chapter 9 identified the major cost elements of ACP programs. The first three—planning and development, recruitment and assessment, and counseling and mentoring—are *institutional* costs that must be borne by the college. The others are *student* costs:

- Tuition/learning materials/supplies
- Student/family living costs
- Transportation
- Childcare

In Stage 1 of the ACP program, the student attends college full-time rather than working. Consequently, the four elements listed above must be provided through personal savings, family support, or aid obtained from federal, state, or community sources. Few ACP candidates, or their families, will be able to provide the necessary support. That leaves federal, state, and community agencies and organizations, which, for the vast majority of ACP students, will be the primary sources of aid.

Chapters 10 and 11 explored federal and state policies and revenue sources. This chapter looks at the local community to find financial and "in kind" resources. Combining the resources of the community college with those available from organizations within its service area can yield large dividends at minimal cost.

This chapter provides advice for ACP coordinators, but it also speaks to the urgency that communities and private organizations should see in supporting adult education programs such as ACP. Every community is shaped by the success of it citizens. Every community should want *all* of its citizens to be productive. Citizens without good job skills not only waste their own talents but can become a liability that must be supported, in part, with tax revenues. The challenge to the community is to mobilize its support base so that unemployed and underemployed adults can be empowered to reach their potential as productive citizens. The resources are there. Every community, regardless of size and overall socioeconomic level, has resources that can be used to complement state and federal aid.

CATEGORIES OF COMMUNITY SUPPORT FOR ACP STUDENTS

Local support for ACP programs can come from three types of organizations: service providers; local organizations that provide funds to service providers; and city, county, and community organizations. In this section, we will examine what those entities have to offer, why they should recognize the value of ACP programs, and how they are best approached to win their support.

1. Service Providers

In this book, the term *service providers* refers to organizations that recruit and coordinate volunteers to provide services such as transportation; childcare; meals; ESL, literacy, and GED training; and personal counseling. Following are examples.

Faith-based organizations

Faith-based organizations include churches, temples, synagogues, and mosques. In any given community, these entities often constitute the first tier in providing benevolent services to people in need. There is also a second tier of faith-based organizations, often national or international in scope, whose activities include educational components. Examples include Campus Crusade for Christ (www.ccci.org), Hillel (www.hillel.org), and Arab World and Islamic Resources (www.awaironline.org). Faith-based organizations support worthy causes both financially and—perhaps more important for ACP programs—through the volunteer activities of their members and supporters. Financial support is an essential component of the ACP concept, and many faith-based organizations have the resources and motivation to support adult learners in that area. But an equally essential component is the "in kind" contributions that those organizations can make by mobilizing the skills and talents of their members. Faith-based organizations can also contribute meeting spaces that allow ACP candidates to visit with counselors on familiar turf. Many people who are intimidated at the prospect of going to see a counselor on a college campus would be perfectly comfortable speaking with the same counselor at a neighborhood church.

In many communities, churches have taken on the challenge of improving the lives of the residents in their areas. Many, particularly larger churches, provide job banks, job fairs, career information, and information about training and education. Some provide scholarships, childcare, and tutoring. Services vary according to the size of the church and the importance it places on education and training. Local branches of Catholic Charities USA have been active in providing ESL and GED training, enabling recent immigrants to take the big first step in qualifying for higher-paying jobs. Many churches have financial resources that they would be willing to use to support adult students in ACP programs.

ACP coordinators should become familiar with the faith-based organizations in their communities, so they can know which organizations provide what services. Coordinators should also work with the organizations to ensure that their educational programs are adequate to prepare adults to enter college. Many faith-based organizations have ample numbers of volunteers, including volunteer teachers, but many of those volunteers will require professional development in the area of adult education. The need for professional development for volunteer teachers gives ACP coordinators an opportunity to create synergy and a sense of shared mission between faith-based organizations and the local colleges that would provide the training.

Friendship West Baptist Church in South Dallas provides a good example of how a single faith-based organization can make a significant difference in the community. The church's website (http://www.friendshipwest.org/) often lists upcoming job fairs and that could be of interest to ACP candidates. The church recently sponsored a communitywide summit on poverty in which representatives from local educational, medical, and social services institutions convened for two days to explore ways to help needy families and adults. The summit generated several initiatives and helped establish the church as a clearinghouse for assistance for the disadvantaged.

One might assume that state-run colleges, which include virtually every community college in the country, are hesitant to work with faith-based organizations. But that is not the case. Many colleges recognize the overlap between their missions and the missions of faith-based organizations and are open to opportunities to collaborate. Our college (Cedar Valley in Dallas) stays in close contact with area churches through campus employees who are members. Those people are encouraged to keep the college's student services department informed about their adult education activities.

Local Chapters of Adult-Empowerment Organizations

This category includes chapters of national organizations such as the National Urban League (http://www.nul.org/) and local nonprofit organizations established to empower career-limited adults through civic engagement, economic self-sufficiency, and education. For example, the Urban League of the Central Carolinas, headquartered in Charlotte, North Carolina, offers a six-week Professional Adult Empowerment Program (PEP) designed to help career-limited adults. Figure 12-1 presents information provided on the organization's website. The intended beneficiaries are the same as those for ACP—adults who are out of work or are working in jobs that do not meet their needs.

Another example is the Wilson Community Improvement Association (WCIA) in Wilson, North Carolina. The organization's website provides this overview:

> Wilson Community Improvement Association (WCIA) was organized in 1968 as a nonprofit neighborhood organization with the expressed purpose of empowering grassroots African-Americans of Wilson, North Carolina, to become self-sufficient through increased education, job training, and economic development by forming partnerships throughout the community. Since its incorporation in 1973, WCIA has addressed such issues as health, job creation, housing, crime, education, and leadership development. . . . WCIA has partnered with more then twenty corporations, foundations, and state and federal institutions that have created 285 units of housing for senior citizens, low and moderate income persons, self-help projects, and job training programs. WCIA created over 300 jobs and has assisted approximately 100 at-risk teenagers through job training. The CDC's existing programs include affordable housing, housing and family counseling, comprehensive senior citizens programs and services, youth mentoring and life survival skills training, job creation, development training and retention, and community leadership training and development. *(http://www.ruralisc.org/wcia.htm)*

Again, we see that the organization's goals and activities are consistent with those of ACP.

Professional Adult Empowerment Program (PEP)

Program Overview—The Professional Adult Empowerment Program is a 6-week program designed especially for underserved adults (low-skilled and/or un/underemployed). Entrance Requirements for participants are a ninth-grade reading level, un/underemployed and a pretest in computer skills. The program offers the following technology skills training and professional development classes:

- **Microsoft's Unlimited Potential Learning Curriculum**. The Microsoft Unlimited Potential course offerings contains many examples of practical, real-world applications covering computer basics, word processing, spreadsheets, databases, presentations, Internet and e-mail and digital media
- **Financial literacy training** using Wachovia's eCommunities curriculum focusing on money management, establishing and managing credit, loans and homeownership

Empowerment/Life Skills combines self-improvement, personal development, and career development training using a holistic approach to enhance participants' attitudes and confidence. Personal counseling is available on an as-needed basis.

Internship (two weeks, optional) An integral part of the program is a two-week, unpaid internship that the participants experience at local businesses or organizations such as Coca-Cola, The American Red Cross, The Department of Social Services, and The JobLink Center. The internship allows the participants the opportunity: (1) to use the skills they have acquired during classroom training; (2) to gain hands-on experience in the office environment; and, (3) to receive instant feedback on their performances. The students are treated as employees and assigned training-related work.

BENEFITS
SHORT-TERM TRAINING • CERTIFICATES AWARDED FOR EACH CLASS COMPLETED • TWO-WEEK INTERNSHIP • JOB PLACEMENT ASSISTANCE CONTINUING EDUCATION UNITS

Preparation And Skills Success (PASS)
PASS is an enrichment program for individuals who score below the ninth grade on the reading comprehension pretest. The program uses instructor-led, customized computer-based training that prepares participants for the (PEP) program. Keyboard training will be available to participants who have limited or no typing skills.

Figure 12-1. Professional Adult Empowerment Program (PEP), Urban League of the Central Carolinas, Charlotte, North Carolina
(http://www.urbanleaguecc.org/programs/workforce.asp#Professional)

Some organizations are designed to meet the special needs of groups such as women and minorities. Examples are the Christian Women's Job Corp and AVANCE (avance.org), an organization that focuses on the needs of poor Latino families in underserved communities.

These examples do not represent isolated phenomena. Organizations of this kind are quite common. Many American communities can boast of similar initiatives. One reaction to this fact might be to assume that, if adult-empowerment programs already exist, the need for ACP may not be so great after all. But that is a misperception. Existing initiatives tend to work independently, often unaware of one another, and they present a bewildering maze that many career-limited adults find intimidating and confusing. The job of the ACP coordinator, as envisioned in this book, would be to bring like-minded organizations together to explore ways to collaborate in providing comprehensive assistance packages to struggling adults.

Community Adult Education Services

Many ACP candidates will require adult basic education, GED, and/or ESL training *before* they are able to enter college programs. ACP coordinators should become familiar with the numerous national (and international) organizations that support education in those areas. See the appendix for a short list of service providers.

Public Libraries

Public libraries, even small ones, routinely provide information on locally offered courses in topics such as adult basic literacy, ESOL (English to speakers of other languages), citizenship, and basic computing. In some cases the courses are offered at the libraries themselves, which provide central locations and easy access. ACP coordinators should establish good working relationships with the public libraries in their communities, and even those in surrounding communities. This will facilitate the free flow of information and enable similar programs to pool their resources.

Public School Districts

Another valuable resource in adult education is the public school system. School systems often provide GED training, as well as adult basic literacy and ESOL courses. School systems welcome opportunities to collaborate with local community and technical colleges, for example, by providing space for adult education classes on evenings and weekends. Since most community colleges are closely allied to the public school systems in their service areas, ACP coordinators should find abundant opportunities to establish contacts among public school teachers and administrators.

Other Community-Based Organizations

Community-based educational organizations are typically nonprofit entities that support education as a primary focus, sometimes in collaboration with public schools. A good example is the Association for Non-Traditional Students in Higher education (ANTSHE), an "international partnership of students, academic professionals, institutions, and organizations whose mission is to encourage and coordinate support, education, and advocacy for the adult learner" (http://www.antshe.org/). The support provided by organizations such as ANTSHE includes scholarship opportunities for adults, networking opportunities for adult students with employers and faculty, career enhancement counseling, and academic degree planning.

In general, community-based organizations focus on short-term, entry-level, and emergency assistance. The ACP coordinator should meet with representatives of each organization to explain the purpose of ACP, what assistance ACP students require, how that assistance can be coordinated with the ACP program, and the mutual benefits of collaboration. In most cases, the assistance provided by community-based organizations will consist of transportation, childcare (through all stages of the ACP program), and training (adult basic literacy, ESL, and GED) for ACP candidates who are not ready for Stage 1.

Individual Development Accounts

Community organizations and individuals can assist in providing matching funds for individual development accounts (IDA). IDAs, special savings accounts for people with low incomes, function like employer-supported savings plans. Money saved by account holders is matched by funds obtained from sources such as government agencies, private companies, churches, and local charities. IDA savings and match money can be used to buy houses, pay for education, or start small businesses. In addition to matching dollars, IDA programs typically help participants learn about budgeting, saving, and banking through financial education classes. Any individual, organization, or business can contribute match dollars to IDAs. In most cases, donors can claim tax deductions for contributions.

2. Local Entities That Provide Funds to Service Providers

This group includes local foundations, charities, and individual benefactors. Successful businesses and individuals often seek opportunities to support their communities through philanthropic initiatives, especially (in the case of businesses) if those initiatives ultimately increase their own profits. One of the premises of this book is that, if businesses can be made to see that supporting the ACP concept will increase their access to well-qualified technicians, they will support it.

A good example of a nonprofit funding organization is the Cooper Foundation of Waco, Texas, whose stated mission is "to make Waco a better or more desirable city in which to live" (http://www.cooperfdn.org/). The foundation realizes this mission through "support of experimental projects, research, surveys, and special community needs for which normal financing is not available." The Cooper Foundation is typical of many local organizations whose missions include funding the development of strategies and programs for adult learners—which is also the mission of ACP. For information on similar organizations, the ACP coordinator can consult publications and websites such as *The Chronicle of Philanthropy* (http://www.philanthropy.com/), the Lumina Foundation (http://www.luminafoundation.org/), and the Wallace Foundation (http://www.wallacefoundation.org/).

Other potential sources of support include "community foundations" such as the Dallas Foundation (dallasfoundation.org), which manages donor-advised funds and field of interest funds.

Many local nonprofit organizations have the capacity to leverage volunteer service and support. Some may also be inclined to provide scholarships for ACP students.

3. City, County, and Community Organizations

This group includes chambers of commerce, business leagues, industrial foundations, and other economic development organizations. One of the primary interests of those organizations is to ensure that the businesses in their communities (both existing and future) have access to adequate numbers of well-trained workers. Consequently, they will look favorably on workforce development initiatives such as ACP and should be willing to become involved in ACP programs. Specifically, they could help to recruit employer partners, ACP student candidates, and organizations to develop scholarship funds. They could also help by supporting state and federal grant requests; persuading city, county, and community organizations to support ACP initiatives; and leading local capital campaigns.

WHY COMMUNITIES AND COMMUNITY AND FAITH-BASED ORGANIZATIONS SHOULD SUPPORT ACP PROGRAMS

Part of the ACP coordinator's job is to sell the ACP concept, that is, to help communities and their nonprofit organizations to see the value of ACP programs and to persuade them to provide support, both financial and "in kind." One way the coordinator can do this is to emphasize the similarities between the goals of ACP programs and the goals of many nonprofits and virtually all faith-based organizations. Like ACP programs, those organizations are dedicated to the betterment of people's lives, especially the lives of people who need a second chance and are willing to work hard to better their circumstances. Broadly speaking, ACP programs accomplish the following three goals, all of which should appeal to most community and faith-based organizations.

- *ACP programs provide a means to reach out to the less fortunate.* ACP programs are designed to help people in ways that will enable them to help themselves. Obviously, this is also one of the strongest motivating factors in the agendas of community and faith-based organizations. Though many have their hands full already, most should be willing to meet with ACP coordinators to explore ways to collaborate in meeting common goals. Through this process, ACP coordinators may also be able to establish relationships with individual benefactors who would be willing to contribute to scholarship funds.
- *ACP programs have the potential to get people off of welfare roles and out of tax-supported institutions such as welfare and corrections.* Homelessness and crime are problems in every community in the country. The potential of ACP programs to alleviate those problems should appeal to community leaders, policymakers, and even individual taxpayers. This aspect of ACP should also appeal to foundations and faith-based organizations that have the resources to fund scholarships.
- *ACP programs can improve the economic and social well-being of any city or community by improving the skills of its workforce.* This message is important to the business community, to economic development organizations, and to chambers of commerce.

THE ROLE OF THE ACP COORDINATOR: A PERSONAL EXPERIENCE

A key part of the ACP coordinator's role is to give adult students the confidence to resume their educations. Many adults feel that they were defeated by the educational system and they are afraid to go back to school. While being sensitive to those emotions, the ACP coordinator must be able to persuade students to "get over it" and move on.

Unless you work every day with struggling adults, it's hard to imagine how fearful some of them are at the prospect of enrolling in college classes. I (Pam) can still vividly remember an incident that took place several years ago at Cedar Valley College, where I have worked for a number of years. A young man was sent to me because he had not been able to pass the assessment exam. (He wasn't disabled, he just couldn't read.) He had scored so low in reading that even the lowest of our remedial classes would have been too difficult. He was obviously uncomfortable and embarrassed by his poor performance and seemed restless and uneasy in my office. When I told him, as gently as I could, that his reading skills were poor and that even our lowest courses would not help him, he suddenly became angry.

"Look, Miss . . . you don't know anything about me," he said in a tense voice. "I have dreamed of going to your college for years. For the past two months, I have come here almost every night and sat in my car in the parking lot and watched the students come and go. Today I finally got up the nerve to come in and ask for help. Now you're tellin' me I don't belong here? That you can't do nothin' for me? Please don't send me away!"

I was stunned by his confession, and knew I had to honor his courage. We were able to get the man get into a literacy program offered by a local church, and we also referred him to a GED program at our outreach center. He left with the satisfaction of knowing that he had taken the first step toward a brighter future. With help, he overcame his anxieties and lack of confidence and saw first-hand that the college and the community were willing to invest in his success.

Identifying potential ACP students and helping them overcome their "higher education anxiety" is the first step in building a robust pipeline of adult learners. Many institutions overlook this factor, even though for many career-limited adults it is the single greatest barrier separating them from success in higher education. Adults who have no experience in higher education often find college campuses so intimidating that they can't bring themselves to walk through the door. For them, it's easier to settle for the "daily bread" they can obtain through menial labor or public assistance than it is to venture into unfamiliar territory and embark on a process that may not bear fruit for several years. If asked about his or her reluctance to go back to school, an adult might say, "I don't belong there," or "They (meaning the college or institution) don't want me," or even, "I really don't know what to say or what to ask for." In years of teaching low-income, first-generation adult students, I have found that the most difficult problem to overcome is the persistent feeling of not belonging in the college classroom. For many adults, that anxiety is compounded by the fact that no one in their immediate families went to college.

The personal anecdote with which I began this section may seem far-fetched, but it's true. It really happened, and I have since come to the conclusion that it represents a widespread phenomenon. When it comes to reentering the world of education, the fears of many adults are extreme and debilitating. As one experienced counselor recently put it, "The situation is worse than you can possibly imagine." The ACP coordinator must work hard to defuse those fears and instill in potential ACP students an understanding that the college and community are on their side.

MAKING SENSE OF THE MAZE

Although virtually every community has organizations that provide services to adult learners, those services are often scattered, isolated, and poorly advertised. To the people who need them, they can look like a rat's maze—with more dead ends than viable pathways.

Part of the ACP coordinator's role is to act as a clearinghouse for information about local resources for adult students. One effective way to approach the task is to ask questions. Here are examples.

- What services are currently available for adult students?
- How does an average person go about finding resources that will help him or her move in the direction of a better career and life?
- How can the relevant services be accessed and coordinated in such a way that they benefit both the recipient and the provider, as well as the community in general? (In other words, what can the ACP coordinator do to ensure that the giving and receiving of assistance create a win-win situation? This is essential to maintaining support among partners and service providers.)

In formulating answers to these and similar questions, the ACP coordinator will make significant strides in determining what services are available and how they can best be used.

ACP coordinators should maintain up-to-date lists of community resources. For many ACP candidates, the coordinators will be the primary points of contact, especially early in the ACP process. The coordinators must be ready to help ACP candidates build the support structures that will enable them to pursue their educational goals.

PUTTING THE PACKAGE TOGETHER

The first part of this chapter described community, faith-based, and other local organizations that can provide support to returning adult students. The information provided is just a starting point. Every community is unique, and every ACP coordinator's list of "go to" organizations will be unique.

"Putting the package together" will require the coordination of services provided by community and faith-based organizations with services provided by the community college. The latter will include financial aid, advisement, tutoring, support groups, student organizations, childcare, and career centers, among others. Having identified all available resources, the coordinator should then begin to develop personal contacts with key individuals at the relevant organizations. Putting together assistance packages—which will vary from student to student—is a collaborative process that will require the efforts of people representing all of the participating organizations.

Here are some practical *do's* and *don't's* that ACP coordinators should follow as they endeavor to recruit and advise students and assemble assistance packages:

Don't . . .

. . . sit in an office and wait for the students to come to you. This may work for traditional students, but most adult students need a little extra encouragement. There may be more adult students than you know sitting out in the parking lot with no idea of how to start.

. . . expect potential ACP students to make their own way through the maze of college registration and enrollment. Adult students often feel intimidated by colleges and their confusing rules and jargon. Because they are older than traditional students, they are sometimes embarrassed to ask obvious questions, such as "How do I read this catalogue?"

. . . send anyone away without at least some type of help. Sending an inquiring adult away with a "sorry, can't help you" means sending him or her away forever. Somewhere in your community is a person or agency that can help this person.

. . . overstay your welcome. ACP coordinators should be sensitive to the limitations on the ability of an organization to support adult students. Be careful not to tap the same source too often. A certain portion of the ACP coordinator's routine should be devoted to looking for new sources.

Do . . .

. . . go where adult students are; don't wait for them to find you. Continuing education and basic skills courses in public schools, libraries, and outreach centers are good places to meet adult students in anxiety-free surroundings.

. . . provide a "safe" place on campus where adult students can gather for advisement. The space does not have to be large or fancy. However, it should create a welcoming environment and should be large enough that the ACP coordinator can speak privately with individuals. It should have one or more tables where students can read informational items and do paperwork. It should have one or more computers with Internet access and a printer, and should provide shelves and bulletin boards for printed items. Ideally, the space would be furnished with a coffee maker and would have a "casual corner," furnished with a couch and one or two comfortable chairs, so that guests sense that part of the space is for work, the other for friendly conversation.

. . . be ready to help any adult student navigate the difficult waters of government programs. This requires being well informed and ensuring that the relevant printed materials are always on hand. The "safe space" referred to in the previous paragraph should be well stocked with information on resources for adult students. Informational items should include contact names and numbers as well as clear, step-by-step instructions for seeking assistance.

. . . be proactive—look for ways to create win-win situations that improve the quality of the local workforce while giving adults the tools to achieve personal success. The ACP concept has the potential to transform communities and the lives of individuals. But someone has to get out and spread the word. That's the ACP coordinator's job. ACP coordinators cannot wait for the community to come to them. They must go into the community.

. . . be creative in finding ways to communicate the ACP concept to special populations. For example, many potential ACP candidates don't read well. To reach out to those people, ACP coordinators should consider producing DVDs about ACP program opportunities, to be placed in easily accessible spaces such as public libraries.

APPENDIX: PROVIDERS OF RESOURCES AND INFORMATION THAT SUPPORT ADULT LITERACY AND ESL EDUCATION

(Adapted from the website of the National Assessment of Adult Literacy, http://nces.ed.gov/naal. Go to "Additional Resources," then "Related Links" and "National Websites.")

America's Literacy Directory (ALD) (www.literacydirectory.org) – a national directory of literacy service providers

Center for Adult English Language Acquisition (www.cal.org/caela) – assists states and communities with high populations of ESL learners

Center for Applied Linguistics (CAL) (www.cal.org) – activities include research, teacher education, analysis and dissemination of information, design and development of instructional materials, technical assistance, conference planning, program evaluation, and policy analysis

Community Technology Centers Network (www.ctcnet.org) – a network of more than 1000 organizations committed to improving the educational, economic, cultural, and political life of their communities through technology

Correctional Education Association (CEA) (www.ceanational.org) – a nonprofit professional association that assists educators and administrators in providing services to students in correctional settings

Equipped for the Future (EFF) (eff.cls.utk.edu) – a national educational improvement initiative for adult basic education and English language learning

Gateway to Educational Materials (www.thegateway.org) – provides information on federal, state, university, nonprofit, and commercial internet sites sponsored by the Department of Education; includes resources on adult education and ESL

Literacy & Learning Disabilities (ldlink.coe.utk.edu) – a clearinghouse for information on issues pertaining to education for people with learning disabilities

Literacy USA (www.naulc.org) – a national alliance of literacy coalitions representing over 4400 literacy providers

National Adult Education Professional Development Association (NAEPDC) (www.naepdc.org) – provides professional development, policy analysis, and information pertaining to adult education

National Center for Family Literacy (NCFL) (www.famlit.org) – services include professional development for practitioners who work in children's education, adult education, ESL, and related literacy fields

National Center for the Study of Adult Learning & Literacy (NCSALL) (www.ncsall.net) – a federally funded research and development center focused solely on adult learning, including English language skills

National Center on Adult Literacy (ncal.literacy.upenn.edu/ncal.html) – performs a variety of services pertaining to adult literacy

Office for Literacy & Outreach Services (http://www.ala.org/ala/olos/literacyoutreach.htm) – promotes literacy and equity of information access initiatives for traditionally underserved populations, including new and nonreaders, people who are geographically isolated, people with disabilities, rural and urban poor people, and people who are generally discriminated against because of race, ethnicity, sexual orientation, age, language, and/or social class

ProLiteracy Worldwide (www.proliteracy.org) – an international nonprofit literacy organization that sponsors educational programs for career-limited adults

Voice for Adult Literacy United for Education (www.valueusa.org) – strengthens adult literacy efforts in the United States through learner involvement and leadership

Helping Karla Succeed

Dick Hinckley

In this book's prologue we introduced Karla, a 24-year-old single mother who was living with her parents. Karla knew she had made some poor choices and she wanted a second chance. In Chapter 8, we provided an update on Karla, showing how an ACP program in telecommunication was helping her to get back on the right track toward a rewarding career and a bright future.

Karla was fortunate that in the six years between her graduation from high school and the time she began her ACP program, the education and business leaders in her town had come together to improve local opportunities for young adults and, at the same time, to meet the region's need for skilled workers. Karla was also fortunate that the telecommunication company to which she applied, unsuccessfully, referred her to the local community college. That referral led her to an ACP program that provided the services she needed to succeed. She was given a second chance and she took it.

Karla had no money for tuition, and she needed help with childcare and transportation. Those needs were met through a combination of Pell Grant dollars, "in-kind" services provided by members of a local church, and a small grant from the Community Education Foundation. The college provided the encouragement and counseling that Karla needed to stay focused and on track. Even when Karla's father suffered a heart attack and was out of work for a period of time, the ACP coordinator was able to arrange for her to take time off to help her mother.

With the help of her community, Karla eliminated her academic deficiencies, significantly improved her employability and job entry skills, and (for the first time in years) began to feel good about herself. As she progressed upward along her ACP program's career ladder, her skills steadily improved. She was acquiring attitudes that would help her to learn throughout her life.

An ACP program helped Karla transition into a rewarding career that will lead her to financial independence.

WHAT WAS GOING ON BEHIND THE SCENES THAT GAVE KARLA HER SECOND CHANCE?

In our Karla scenario, we have focused mostly on *her*. But that's only one part of the story. If people in Karla's circumstances are to be given the second chance they deserve, much work has to be done behind the scenes. In a sense, that is the topic of this book—the hard work that must be done to ensure that when the Karlas across our nation begin ACP programs, everything is in place and ready to go.

Let's look at what went on behind the scenes in Karla's case.

For years, Medford High School had an excellent Tech Prep program that was articulated with Grayslake Community College. The Medford-Grayslake Tech Prep Consortium was diligently reevaluating its programs, having become convinced that Career Pathways (CP) offered the best model for involving business and industry in strengthening the employability of their students. Over time, the consortium's curriculum committee essentially rewrote the program's high school and community college curricula, using cluster-specific industry needs as a guide. While Tech Prep had been available when Karla was in school, she had not taken advantage of the program.

Meanwhile, Medford community leaders and the Rock Ridge County Economic Development Council (RRCEDC) were increasingly alarmed at the number of job openings that couldn't be filled. The shortage of well-trained workers had become so acute that several local companies were planning to leave Medford and the county. At the same time, more and more of Medford's young people were looking outside the community for their futures. These issues concerned Grayslake's president and her board members, several of whom were local business owners.

The president called a meeting at her office and invited a few business leaders, Medford's mayor, and the director of RRCEDC. Recognizing the need for a bold new approach, they formed a small working group to lay out their plans.

Using resources in the college and information provided by RRCEDC, the working group developed profiles of the region's industry sectors. The group identified healthcare, telecommunication, and financial services as the industries with the greatest potential to lead the region in an ACP effort. The following overall support structure was proposed:

Adult Career Pathways Consortium
Business Task Group *College Services and Instruction Task Group* *Community Task Group* *Community Education Foundation*

Business Task Group *– With the assistance of a consulting group, the consortium convened CEOs in the three targeted industries: healthcare, telecommunication, and financial services. Mirroring the process presented in Chapter 4 (see "Convening Business Representatives"), the participants developed career ladders, designed support systems, and drew up the agreements necessary to ensure that all parties were working toward the same goals.*

College Services and Instruction Task Group *– While the business task group was working out the details of the business sector involvement, the college was strengthening its recruitment, advising, and counseling services so that it would be able to attract and meet the needs of ACP target populations. Campus committees took on new roles to improve their ability to work with the targeted populations.*

Community Task Group *– The community task group convened faith-based and community organizations to seek their assistance. Medford had a private foundation, established by a former banker, that was already engaged in support activities for the local public and private schools. Its past activities included the purchase of a bus for special education students, contributions to a health clinic for poor women, and assistance in rebuilding a historic church after it suffered fire damage. The foundation was able to provide support to the ACP program under its mission to help disadvantaged students. It set up a category of funding for ACP to provide last-resort (after state and federal assistance sources were exhausted) childcare and transportation support. Several churches were able to pledge clothing, counseling services, and food bank support.*

Community Education Foundation *– The Community Education Foundation initiative was a key component. It led a capital campaign to raise funds for overall ACP operation and to guarantee every ACP program student two years of tuition, books, and fees (after all other sources of support had been exhausted) at Grayslake Community College. The foundation was able to raise $10 million, which it used to support the new ACP management and support services needed to begin and sustain ACP operations.*

Outreach and Extension *– Since establishing the ACP program, the ACP Consortium has worked with Medford Public Schools to strengthen its CP programs and to drive the industry involvement to the middle schools with tours and other business engagement opportunities. The entire curriculum in math and science has been reevaluated and strengthened with the addition of contextual instruction, improved faculty development, and new 4+2 articulation agreements with state universities.*

A local state legislator became familiar with the program and introduced legislation to provide seed dollars to communities seeking to adopt the Medford model.

IT COULD HAPPEN

Stories like Karla's could happen all across the country, if the right leaders are willing to step forward. For the sake of the many Americans whose circumstances are similar to Karla's, and for the sake of the nation's overall economic health, that leadership is urgently needed and needed now. We have moved the conversation of reform and improvement in career and technical education to a new level, the community. Across this country, we must take charge of our future, community by community. Just as "all politics is local," education reform and business survival are local, too. It is time for action. The Adult Career Pathways concept represents the nexus where business, education, and the community can and must come together to reclaim our young adults and our collective future.